THE
PRIMITIVE CHURCH
OR
THE CHURCH IN THE DAYS
OF THE APOSTLES

THE
PRIMITIVE CHURCH

OR
THE CHURCH IN THE DAYS
OF THE APOSTLES

BY

D. I. LANSLOTS, O.S.B.

WITH A PREFACE BY THE
RT. REV. F. C. KELLEY, D.D.,
BISHOP OF OKLAHOMA

TAN BOOKS AND PUBLISHERS, INC.
Rockford, Illinois 61105

IMPRIMI POTEST

Die 29. Dec. 1925,

Ernestus Helmstetter, O.S.B.

Abbas B. M. Immac. et Præs. Congre. Amer.-Cass.

NIHIL OBSTAT

Sti. Ludovici, die 17. Maii, 1926,

Joannes Rothensteiner

Censor Librorum

IMPRIMATUR

Sti. Ludovici, die 20. Maii, 1926,

✠ *Joannes J. Glennon, D.D,*

Archiepiscopus

Originally published by
B. Herder Book Co., St. Louis, Missouri

Copyright © 1926 by B. Herder Book Co.

Copyright © 1980 by TAN Books and Publishers, Inc.

Library of Congress Catalog No.: 79-67862

ISBN: 0-89555-134-9

Printed and bound in the United States of America

TAN BOOKS AND PUBLISHERS, INC.
P. O. Box 424
Rockford, Illinois 61105

1980

PREFACE

BY

THE RIGHT REV. FRANCIS C. KELLEY, D.D.,
BISHOP OF OKLAHOMA

The man who has inherited a noble name and lives up to it, even though miserably poor in the goods of this world, loves to dwell upon the first heroic gestures with which his line began. The farther he can trace back that line, the more satisfaction and joy does he bring to his study.

Here is a history that tells of the first heroic gestures of what may well be called the Miracle of Christianity's Spread, the first circlet on the tiara of the Church after her ennobling at Pentecost. As members of that Church this is a story we should love and cherish, because it is the story of the beginnings of the line of our spiritual ancestry.

Joubert said that "Religion makes it the duty of the pauper to be liberal, noble, generous, and magnificent in charity." The Church has conferred that nobility on her followers, which is one of the reasons why she changed the face of the world. No one can read the record of her first seventy years without marvelling at the wonder of them in their accomplishments. It is like seeing a statue take form under the hands of the artist.

Here the artist was Charity; but Charity released from the bonds that confined her to one race and given the freedom of the Gospel of Jesus Christ. Poor as were the preachers of Christ crucified, they had His religion, and through it they were liberal, noble, generous, and magnificent with the Charity that is alike the inspiration of the Church and her treasure. The story told in this book is the Peerage of Christianity, its joy and its pride; as well as our own urge to emulate the Apostolic hunger for conquest in Christ's name.

CONTENTS

INTRODUCTION

The period of the Church's history of which this book treats, seems to have a special attraction for our contemporary scientists of all shades. Civil and religious origins are as a field unexplored, appealing especially to modern science: the origin of Christianity and its development are no exception. After Christ had consecrated His teaching with His blood, the Church existed, but to have her fulfil the mission entrusted to her, meant the long and generous work of the Apostles, guided and assisted by the superior power of the Holy Ghost. It is almost impossible to understand Christianity rightly without considering its origin and early development. As embryology is the basis of good and sound physiology, so does the origin of a thing help the study of its development. The problem of the natural or the supernatural of a religion cannot be solved without research into its beginning. The difficulties and obstacles encountered and overcome in the beginning of Christianity furnished our ancient apologists one of their most convincing arguments in favor of its divinity. The activity of Renan and the unbelieving rationalists of our day is aimed especially at undermining the first and second century of Christianity, which period seemed somewhat neglected by our ancient apologists, probably for the reason that it was supposed to be well known. As error in religious matters always invites the attention of the right-minded and brings out the truth, the rationalists have forced Catholics and sincere Protestants alike to reaffirm and to prove the principle of the supernatural. The followers of Strauss and Baur do not consider so much the personality of Christ as the activity of the Apostles in itself and in its consequences. Facts well established must convince even a rationalist; while he may not admit the supernatural, he must give up many of his prejudices. Unbelief is the misfortune, not merely of those who claim that the human mind has no limits and that reason will find some time a natural explanation of any fact, but also of those who admit these false theories without argument or enquiry.

The present-day attitude on the part of many men of so-called science, who follow in the steps of their rationalist confrères, as also the attitude of society in many quarters, is under many respects very similar to what it was when Christianity came to reform and transform it—the world—low morality, the same confusion of ideas, the same hostility to the Church, who is denied not only the rights she claims, but even the rights of any society duly organized. The Church of all times and places feels the need and at the same time the intrinsic power to adapt herself to circumstances; in the face of a world turning to paganism, she realizes the obligation of asserting herself apostolic for self-preservation. She therefore recalls to mind the early days of her existence and the wonders worked by her heroes. The history of the Apostolic Age, from the first Christian Pentecost up to the death of St. John, reveals the Church as the divine Founder left her, and as the Apostles divinely inspired applied the teaching of their Master to the multifarious conditions of society, high and low, at that time.

No one can reasonably lay claim to the name of Christian if his belief and practice have little in common with the teaching of the Apostles. They preached the one faith; the believer in the Bible as the inspired word of God, or even a good philosopher, could not admit more than one faith in matters of religion. God cannot contradict Himself; He cannot but reveal the same identical truths when He addresses them to many.

After admitting that Christ is God, and that His Church will endure up to the end of time, the conclusion cannot be denied that the Church now must be in all essentials the same as she was in the days of the Apostles. The Christian society in the days of the Apostles was one; if any one disagreed with it in matters of faith, he ceased to be a member. There are hundreds of Christian denominations now, all claiming membership in that society, but their claim is absurd because faith is one. With the help of divine Revelation concerning the teaching of the Redeemer, and with the application of that teaching by the Apostles, as recorded in their inspired acts and writings, and with the further assurance that heaven and earth shall pass away, but that Christ's words shall not pass away, any unbiased enquirer after the truth would discover what the standard of present-day faith and morality should be. The history of the Primitive Church must reflect itself in the present-day Church, if it is to be considered the continuation of the Primitive Church. This makes that history of supreme importance to all that lay claims to the name of Christian.

THE AUTHOR

THE PRIMITIVE CHURCH

CHAPTER FIRST

THE CHURCH A PERFECT SOCIETY IN ITS OWN RIGHT

THERE are two powers recognized and established by God for the government of the world—the civil and the religious or ecclesiastical. Some persons are endowed from above with power to govern the commonwealth and to promote the temporal welfare of its citizens; and others to rule the Church of Christ and to procure the spiritual welfare of all mankind. Each of the two powers is supreme in its own right. Does the Church hold her powers of government from the civil authority? Did the Founder of Christianity —Jesus Christ—give authority over it to the civil power? Did the faithful give it? Is the supreme civil authority such that all spiritual matters are subjected to it? Do the peace and prosperity of the commonwealth demand that all authority be concentrated in the civil ruler? The true answers to these questions should settle the relationship between Church and State. If it had been Christ's intention to give to the civil powers authority over His Church, He would have prepared these powers for the task in the same way as He trained His Apostles; He certainly could have done so; but there is not one word nor any indication on Christ's part to that effect. For the first three hundred years there were no temporal rulers, to whom the destinies of the Church could have been entrusted; the Roman emperors were deadly enemies of the Christian religion. The fact that they were not Christians was not an obstacle; the Apostles were not Christians when Christ called them to the apostolate. If Christ had wished to entrust His Church to the tender care of temporal sovereigns, He would have called and instructed them.

The power to govern the Church belongs to the supernatural order, because her existence and her purpose are supernatural. If Christ then has made no exception, the government of the Church cannot belong to a natural and inferior power; no such exception is recorded.

Unity of faith is the supreme law of the Church; this unity cannot be had without God's help, which for the purpose is nowhere promised to secular authorities.

If the government of the Church was by Christ's institution committed to the secular power, the body of the faithful should not only have been informed of it, but such ordinance should have been carried out. History records that the reverse is the case and that whenever the secular authorities assumed any part of ecclesiastical jurisdiction, the Church invariably protested. The secular rulers who gave the best proofs of their devotion to the Church, took good care not to invade the domain of Church government.

That right was not given to them by Christ for their prominence within the Church; the chief secular ruler is not a chief member of the Church on account of his position. Church and State are quite distinct powers, membership of the one does not necessarily mean membership of the other. The chief of a state is not a member of the Church because he is chief, but because he has been baptized. In the Old Testament the government of the synagogue belonged to the priests, not to the kings. The power to rule the Church could not have been conveyed by the faithful, because they themselves did not possess it.

Peace and tranquillity, which are the main purpose of a state, can not be secured without some religious cult, but the conclusion that therefore the whole government of all spiritual and temporal matter is committed to secular rulers goes far beyond the premises. We all need many things to support life, but we are not therefore justified in securing them by infringing the rights of the lawful owners. Peace within a state is necessary to the happiness of its citizens and as it cannot be had without religion, the state should encourage religion, and with its help promote the welfare of the people.

Needless to say that the Church has always resisted the encroachments of secular rulers. St. Ambrose furnishes us a proof of it. Emperor Valentinian II insisted upon obtaining a basilica for the Arians. St. Ambrose told him: "You order me to give up a basilica. My answer is: It is unlawful for me to give it and inexpedient for you to accept it. You can not seize the house of a private citizen and yet you would despoil the Church of God? They say that everything is permissible to the Emperor and that everything belongs to him; I answer: Do not be mistaken, Emperor; imperial rights do not extend to things divine." On another occasion he was cited about a question of faith before lay-judges. He answered the Emperor as follows: "If a bishop is to be taught by a layman, the layman will teach and the bishop will listen; the layman will instruct the bishop. If you remember the Scriptures or olden times you will find that in matters of faith the bishops judge the Christian emperors, but not the emperors the bishops." On a different occasion he reminded the Emperor of the answer his father had given to certain bishops who had asked for permission to assemble in synod. "It does not belong to me," he said, "as a mere layman, to inquire curiously into similar matters; let the priests to whom they belong meet wherever they please." St. Ambrose has given us the answer of the Church to all civil despots, whether he be a Nero, a Napoleon, or a Bismarck.

The Church has always claimed to be a perfect society in her own right and independent of any other society. A society is perfect in itself, when for its scope and for the means to it, it is self-sufficient; such is the case with the Church.

The purpose of her institution is to perpetuate the mission of Christ,—the work of our redemption, and to carry out His plan in regard to our salvation. This purpose is unique and is not subordinated to the end of any other society. The means appointed by Christ to attain the end are self-sufficient. As the Church aims at supernatural blessings, it far excels all civil societies aiming at worldly goods only. The final purpose of the Church is the eternal salvation of souls through supernatural means. The state can aim only at temporal prosperity, which can only indirectly be useful to the salvation of souls.

The Church needs temporal property to carry on her work, but that does not imply that she is destitute of the necessary means to the end. Christ Himself has given power to the Church to acquire the temporal means that may be useful to the end, and has arranged that those who serve the Gospel shall live by the Gospel (1 Cor. IX.14). The fact that the Church needs material help does not make her the inferior of the State, no more than man requiring food becomes inferior to it. We can not conclude from the fact that the State needs the Church, as a promoter and a safeguard of the moral order, that the welfare of the State is the supreme purpose of the Church; not everything that is useful or necessary to another thereby becomes a subordinate means to the other. The Angels help us, yet they rank above us; so is the Church, though helpful to the State, far above it.

All power comes from above; no society can have any authority except it be so given. Christ made His Church a kingdom, that is to say, a perfect society in itself, fully sufficient to itself and not necessarily dependent upon any other; the multitude and diversity of its adherents are quite able to provide the material needs. There is another difference between the kingdom of the Church and any other. No country has the guarantee of permanent independence; it may disintegrate and be absorbed by a more powerful country and become a province. There is no fear of the Church being absorbed by any state, because it is above it, nor by any other spiritual power, because by Christ's institution and promise there can be no other spiritual kingdom upon earth. The government of the Church is different from that of all other states. The spiritual dominion of the Church extends to whatever place may harbor its adherents; the civil power is limited to the citizens within its own confines. The authority of the Church in no way decreases the authority of the State, because it covers matters that are not of the competency of the State.

The study of the first century of the Christian era will furnish the views which the Apostles entertained in theory and in practice concerning the relationship between Church and State. They have taught us by word and example that the Church is a fully self-sufficient society, endowed with all the means required for the salvation of souls (Eph. III.22; IV. 1–11). The Apostles have carried out their mission independently of the civil powers. Their successors have proceeded in the same way, and invariably vindicated the rights of the Church against the most powerful of despots. There can be no society without authority; no kingdom without a king. The Church being a visible society must have a visible head. All admit that Christ after His Ascension remains the invisible head of the Church. Who was the first to be invested by Christ with the supreme authority over the whole Church—the kingdom of Christ upon earth?

CHAPTER SECOND

THE FIRST VISIBLE HEAD OF THE CHURCH
AFTER CHRIST'S ASCENSION

St. Peter is called the Prince of the Apostles, and justly so, because he was appointed by Christ to be the visible head of the Church in preference to the other Apostles. This supremacy in the college of Apostles and in the government of the Church was promised to Peter and to him alone.

The primacy of Peter is one of the revealed truths most clearly recorded in the Bible. In this instance there is much significance in a name. Peter's name had been Simon before. To make it plain that the words of promise apply to Simon exclusively, Christ gave him the name of Peter (Matt. XVI.17–19). When Christ spoke of the rock on which He would build His Church, He designated Peter; Christ speaking in Aramaic called him Kephas, meaning both Peter and rock (Jo. I.42). In Aramaic and also in French the same word designates a person and a rock. In the words of the promise to Peter the metaphor of the foundation is explained by the metaphor of the keys (Matt. XVI.18–19). Christ intended to reward the magnificent profession of faith on the part of Peter with an equally splendid prerogative. He alone

8

makes the profession; he alone receives the reward. Peter alone is called blessed because he alone had been favored by the Father with a special revelation. The primacy promised to Peter concerns the very constitution and the government of the Church. He is not called the foundation of the Church because he worked harder and with greater constancy than the others, but that he may prove himself superior to all attacks. Our Lord says expressly: "The gates of hell shall not prevail against it," that is, against the Church built upon Peter—the rock. That foundation is just as essential to the Church as a foundation is to a house. The foundation comes first in the building process. If we consider the beginning of the Church, all those who first taught the doctrines of the Church and those by whom the Church was propagated are in a sense the foundations of it. With respect to teaching, the Apostles and the Prophets are called the foundation of the Church (Eph. II.20). In regard to the propagation the Apostles are called the foundations (Apo. XXI.14). Foundation, however, signifies more properly the support of the whole building; in that sense Peter alone is the foundation; to Peter as the foundation the Church owes its firmness, not to be shaken by any power whatsoever. No other Apostle is called Peter-rock—and therefore no other supports the whole church as a rock.

Christ in promising the primacy of jurisdiction to Simon, also uses another symbol,—that of the keys (Matt. XVI.19). The keys express the power to administrate and rule. The symbol of the keys like

that of the foundation rock proves that **Peter** was
to be the head and the prince of the Apostles. The
image expresses that the supreme power in the Church
was promised to Peter, to whom all others having keys
would be subject. When Christ afterwards gives to
the other Apostles the power to bind and to loose,
He does not use the metaphor of the keys (Matt.
XVIII.18). They had indeed the power to open
heaven and to shut it, but that power was not supreme
such as would be designated by the keys.

Peter's privilege did not consist in this that he first
of all opened the gates of heaven to the Jews (Acts
II.34–41) and the Gentiles, because this happened
only once and could not be repeated, any more than
that America could have been discovered twice. It
seems ridiculous to imagine that Our Lord made the
solemn promise to Peter simply to signify that he
would exercise the power entrusted to him a little
while before the other Apostles.

The primacy of government is promised to Peter
in the same singular manner as the power to bind
and to loose. To bind does not mean only to declare
that something is illicit, but also to prohibit; to loose
is not only to declare a thing licit, but also to permit
it. Our Lord therefore clearly indicates the fullest
power to govern.

The divinely acquired knowledge and profession of
Christ's divinity distinguished Peter from the other
Apostles; there would have been no difference in the
reward, if the same power had been promised to all.
The illustrations used by Christ clearly show that

greater power is given to Peter. But did not Christ say to Peter: "Go behind me, Satan?" (Matt. XVI. 23). When Peter played the part of a tempter, the primacy had been promised to him, but not conferred. The Apostles themselves may have thought that by those words the promise had been affected, but subsequent events prove that such was not the case. As long as Christ dwelled with His Apostles in a visible manner, Peter, though the first among them, could not claim obedience from them. The prerogatives conferred upon Peter show that some day he would be their visible head. Christ imposed upon him the name of Peter; it can not have been given in vain; it must signify some future event. In the Old Testament the name divinely given to Abram indicated what was to happen to him. Simon the son of Jonas is called Peter—the rock—upon which the Church is to be built; what the foundation is to a building that is the head to a society. Christ is the cornerstone of that spiritual edifice; what Christ was in the institution and will remain forever in an invisible manner, Peter will be, as Christ's vicegerent, in a visible manner.

Christ promised that Peter would be in catching men what he had been in catching fish; Peter had been the chief actor in the miraculous draught. In the Gospel narrative the sea is a picture of the world; the fishes, of men, and the fishermen, of the Apostles. Both Simon and Andrew hear from the lips of the Master: "I will make you to be fishers of men" (Matt. IV.19). Christ made a special promise in the case of Peter: "Fear not: from henceforth thou shalt catch men" (Luke V.10). Simon is exhibited to us as the chief in this fishing party; his ship is chosen, he is ordered to launch out into the deep, and to let down the net. At the sight of the miracle Peter fell down at Jesus' feet; the other Apostles are treated as inferiors; Jesus addresses only Simon. If this material fishing is a picture of spiritual fishing, and if Christ's promise is to be fulfilled, Peter must act as head and chief in this spiritual fishing and among the fishers of men.

Christ prays particularly for Peter that his faith might not fail, so that he could confirm his brethren in the faith after Christ's Ascension. The particular visible mission of Christ among His Apostles is transferred unto Peter. Christ said to him: "Simon, Simon, behold Satan hath desired to have you, that he might sift you as wheat. But I have prayed for thee that thy faith fail not: and thou, being once converted, confirm thy brethren" (Luke XXII.31, 32). All are desired, but Christ prays for one. Praying for one was sufficient, if all were to be confirmed in that one and if all were subject to him; Christ entrusted them all in the time of danger to the care of Peter. Christ prepared Peter more particularly for the charge He put upon him. If Peter is to take the place of Christ, visible head of the Church, he must know Him more intimately and love Him more ardently, because in his official capacity he is to a certain extent one and the same with his Chief.

Peter was the inseparable companion of Christ. Sometimes Christ took Peter, James, and John with Him; often Peter alone was chosen. Christ goes into Peter's ship; he is ordered to cast a hook into the sea, and take from the mouth of the fish to be caught a coin. The same tax is paid for Christ and for Peter (Matt. XVII.26). Peter was with Christ on the water (XIV.29). This intimate companionship must have impressed the other Apostles and prepared them for a recognition of the primacy promised to Peter. When Christ was still on earth, Peter often acted as the leader of the Apostles. In their name he addressed the Master: Behold, we have left all things. Lord, to whom shall we go? (Jo. VI.69). Lord, dost Thou speak this parable to us, or likewise to all? (Luke XII.41). Simon and they that were with him, followed after Him (Mark I.36). In Luke VIII.45 and IX.32 the same expression occurs. This manner of speaking denotes a leader, a chief. Whenever the names of the Apostles are given Peter always heads the list. This is not because he was the oldest, or the first called, because under both respects Andrew ranked first; there could be no other reason than that of his dignity. When Matthew gives the names of the twelve Apostles (X.2) he expressly adds: The first, Peter. When Our Lord reprimands His Apostles for their contention as to who would be the greatest, He condemns domineering and ostentation, but not dignity and authority. We can hardly suppose that there could have been any such contention, unless the Apostles had understood from the words of Christ that they would not be equal, and that Peter was preferred to the others.

After His resurrection Christ gives the proofs that Peter's denial had not caused Him to annul the promise. On the day of Christ's Resurrection the Angel told the women: Go and tell his disciples and Peter (Mark XVI.7). Peter only is mentioned by name that all might understand that his sin had not changed Christ's plan.

Scripture has recorded when the promised primacy was actually conferred on Peter. The risen Christ appeared to His disciples at the lake of Tiberias, and the following conversation ensues between Our Lord and Peter: "Simon, son of John, lovest thou me? He saith to him: Yea, Lord, thou knowest that I love thee. He saith to him: Feed my lambs. He saith to him again: Simon, son of John, lovest thou me? Yea, Lord, thou knowest that I love thee. He saith to him: Feed my lambs. He saith to him the third time: Lovest thou me? And he said to him: Lord, thou knowest all things: thou knowest that I love thee. He said to him: Feed my sheep" (Jo. XXI.15–17). It is evident that Christ's promise had to be fulfilled some time; the above words clearly indicate the fulfilment. Peter is commissioned to feed the whole flock, that is, the universal Church. Christ was about to leave the world and return to heaven. It was proper that the supreme visible head of the Church should be pointed out just as clearly as he had been promised. It could not have been done in clearer terms than those we read in the gospel. A fishing party offered the occasion for the promise and for its fulfilment.

The words quoted above clearly show that to Peter and to Peter alone a special charge is entrusted; that charge could be no other than the supreme power as head of the Apostles, and of the whole Church. To feed the sheep and the lambs is the same as to rule. He is made the shepherd of the flock, of which even the Apostles are members. They will go and deliver the good tidings to all nations; they will have authority over all; Peter alone will be their superior.

Peter understood his mission; the Apostles understood it, and their acts confirm it. Peter presides at the election of a successor to Judas (Acts I.15). Peter is the first to preach the Gospel. The efficacy of his words and the gift of miracles gather the first converts into the fold. Peter plays the chief rôle in the work by visiting all (Acts IX.32). Peter is the first to be warned in a vision that the time had arrived to receive the Gentiles into the Church. The great Apostle of the Gentiles, St. Paul, having been taught by Christ Himself, did not need instruction from Peter or the other Apostles, yet he went to pay his respects to Peter, and remained with him two weeks. Of the other Apostles, he had seen none but James, who was then Bishop of Jerusalem. Peter acted in the council of the Apostles at Jerusalem as head of the Church, and was recognized by the Apostles as such; Peter speaks and all the multitude held their peace, and approved his decision; Paul and James speak, but only to uphold Peter's infallible judgment in matters of faith and morals (Acts XV. 7–12).   Christ gave a visible head to the Church in the person of Peter in order to effect and to preserve its unity.   By making Peter the foundation He made him the supreme ruler; by giving to him the keys of the kingdom of heaven He made him the supreme dispenser; by entrusting the whole flock to his care He made him the chief shepherd.   Peter is so appointed that he might do in a visible way what Christ does for His Church in an invisible manner. As the Church is to last unto the end of time as Christ established it, so there must always be a visible head.

The above considerations are all the more important, as without them it would be impossible to form an idea of the Church, as Christ founded it.

A few occurrences in the days of which we write might, if misunderstood, throw a shadow upon the primacy of Peter.

The first of these is the mission of Peter to Samaria. Philip the Deacon, when expelled from Jerusalem in the persecution that followed the death of St. Stephen, proceeded north and converted many Samaritans to the faith.   When the Apostles, who remained in Jerusalem, heard this, they sent unto them Peter and John (Acts VIII.14).   Can we argue from that fact that the college of Apostles was superior to Peter? We must distinguish a mission by authority from a mission by request.   If Peter was sent by a superior, we must admit that Peter was not the superior.   To understand how he was sent, we must remember his position as explained above. The Bible abundantly proves that all missions do not imply inferiority. What Christian will admit that the Son is inferior to the Father, because He was sent by Him into this world? We read in the book of Josue (XXII) that the children of Israel sent on a mission Phinees the priest and ten others, each a chief of one of the tribes. Again we read (Acts XV) that when the question of circumcision was raised for the converted Gentiles, the faithful at Antioch sent Paul and Barnabas to consult the Apostles in Jerusalem. The great Jewish historian Josephus records that the Jews sent their high-priest Ismael on a mission to Emperor Nero in Rome. Why did the Apostles request Peter to go when the other Apostles might have done just as well? The sacred text does not give the reasons, but we may suppose that the old ill-feeling between the Samaritans and the Jews demanded the presence of the chief of the Apostles to overcome all resistance and objections on either side. It is as in the physical order; the more the various elements tend to repel each other, the greater must be the power in the principle to obtain cohesion. Another reason may have been that the presence of the chief was required to offset the nefarious efforts of Simon the Magician. Simon had preceded Philip in Samaria, and gave himself out as some great one (Acts VIII). Simon was one of Philip's converts; but his desire to buy the power to give the Holy Ghost showed that he could not be depended upon. His heart was not right in the sight of God. One endowed with supreme authority was required to paralyze the seductions of this sovereign impostor. Supposing, however, that Peter went by request, why was John sent with him? John certainly was not the superior of the other Apostles. This is not the first instance when Peter and John went together. They appear together in the cure of the lame man and after that before the Sanhedrim; Peter plays the chief rôle, even when in the company of St. John. Far from proving anything against the primacy the mission to Samaria rather confirms it.

Another objection may be found in the rebuke administered to Peter by the newly converted Jews in Jerusalem, after he had received Gentiles into the Church without circumcision: "Why didst thou go to men uncircumcised, and didst eat with them? (Acts XI.3). Peter explains to them the vision of Cornelius and his own. Peter is called to task; he humbly submits, therefore he was not the chief; is that conclusion good logic? Who are the remonstrants in this case? Not the Apostles, but the new converts from Judaism, who had not abandoned their views of superiority over the Gentiles. Is Peter their inferior? Is the rebuke administered to him one in the odious sense of the word? This is not clear from the text. In the supposition that it was taken very seriously, would the rebellion prove anything against the primacy? It is only a repetition of what happened to Aaron (Numbers XVI). He had been appointed by God as the high-priest, yet there were

some who with Core, Dathan, and Abiron objected
and coveted the dignity for themselves. But was the
objection to Peter's act so serious, when his accusers,
after hearing his explanation, held their peace and
glorified God saying: "God then hath also to the
Gentiles given repentance unto life" (Acts XI.18).
You may further say: Peter at any rate had to render
an account and this could not be demanded except of
an inferior or an equal. I would answer you: You
then make Peter an inferior to or an equal of the first
converts of the Church in Jerusalem; you prove too
much, therefore you prove nothing. When Mary
and Joseph had lost Jesus, they, on finding Him in
the temple, said to Him: Son, why hast thou done
so to us? (Luke II.48). Jesus explains his act.
Does that make Him the inferior or the equal of
Mary and Joseph? Often in the Old Testament God
Himself has given an account of His acts by the
mouth of His prophets.

The letter of St. Paul to the Galatians presents
another difficulty. The purpose of that letter is two-
fold; first, to refute the common error of converted
Jews clinging to their traditions; secondly, to claim
for himself the prerogatives of a true Apostle, as
the Twelve chosen by Christ. These converts entertained misgivings about Paul and his mission. Paul
compares himself with Peter, and claims that as Peter
is the Apostle of the circumcision, so he is the Apostle
of the Gentiles. Some pretended that Paul was not a
true Apostle, and that his teaching did not conform
to that of the other Apostles. Paul refutes both

assertions. Having received the apostolate shortly after his conversion from Christ Himself, he felt no need of any instruction or mission from the Apostles in Jerusalem. He went immediately to work in Arabia, then returned to Damascus and only after three years went to see Peter in Jerusalem. After fourteen years he returned to Jerusalem with Barnabas and Titus, by divine command. Some converts refused to receive Titus, because he was not circumcised. Titus, however, was received, which proves that there was no difference of opinion between Paul and the other Apostles. The argument of Paul was not with Peter or the other Apostles, but with some converts from Judaism. So far nothing is proved against the primacy of Peter; but in that same letter Paul writes as follows: "When Cephas was come to Antioch, I withstood him to the face, because he was to be blamed" (Gal. II.11). Do not these words argue against the primacy of Peter? The Council of Jerusalem had exempted the Gentiles from the observance of the Mosaic law, and had also recognized the apostolate of Paul, but some questions had not been settled, such as, whether the law of Moses was still binding on the Jews after the coming of Christ; whether the Gentiles had to become Jews before their reception into the Church. The feelings of the converted Jews were well known and for argument's sake it is immaterial whether the meeting of Peter and Paul occurred before or after the Council of Jerusalem. Peter used to eat with the Gentiles, but when some messengers came from James, the Bishop of Jerusalem, Peter discontinued the practice for fear of scandalizing those of the circumcision. Here was the case of dissimulation on the part of Peter. Paul mentions the occurrence for the only purpose of convincing the faithful of Galatia that the gospel of liberty, which he preached was the true gospel, to which even Peter after a few moments of weakness yielded. There is no question of a dogmatic disagreement between the two Apostles. How could there be, as Peter himself had had a divine revelation on the subject? Peter had baptized the heathen Cornelius without submitting him to any Jewish rite; in the Council of Jerusalem he had proclaimed salvation by grace, not by the law; he had opposed the pretention of the Jewish converts that Titus should be circumcised; he had recognized the apostolate of Paul. Peter perhaps looked for such an opportunity to settle the question of circumcision for good and for ever. It is easy to imagine the predicament of Peter, when he had to choose between the opposition of Paul, and the newly arrived zealots from Jerusalem. Peter appeared to waver and was to blame; Paul won the day, but there was no question of primacy or doctrine; it was simply a question of expediency, until it was finally settled. The opponent of Peter is the same Paul who, after the Council of Jerusalem, passed through Iconium and Lystris with Timothy, and circumcised him, because of the Jews who were in those places (Acts XVI.3). Paul knew from his own experience that there is a difference between principles and their application; he knew that circumstances must be taken into consideration. It is undeniable that Paul rebuked Peter. Did he do so because he considered himself Peter's superior? Certainly not. Paul called himself the least of the Apostles. But a brotherly correction may and must be made sometimes, even by an inferior. Paul may be praised for his courage; Peter, for his sincere humility. The occurrence shows that Paul looked upon Peter as an extraordinary man.

CHAPTER THIRD

THE FIRST PENTECOST

The Acts of the Apostles are, together with their Epistles, the inspired history of the Primitive Church, in the same way as the Gospels are the inspired version of the life and the teaching of Christ up to His glorious Ascension into Heaven.

During the forty days after His Resurrection Christ had repeatedly presented Himself to the Apostles in visible form; He had eaten with them; He had spoken to them of the kingdom of God. This kingdom meant the advent of the Messiah, by Whom the worship of the true God had been reëstablished; it meant the religion of Christ and all things that belong to it, that is, the whole economy of the New Law, or in other words the Church founded by Christ. Christ had commanded them not to leave Jerusalem, but to wait for the promise of the Father—the coming of the Holy Ghost. The Apostles still shared the opinion, common among the Jews at that time, that the Messiah would reign upon earth for the greater glory and happiness of the Jewish race. When questioned by them, Christ in His reply rebukes them and insinuated that His kingdom is a spiritual kingdom, to be spread over the whole world through faith, not by the sword. Christ appeared a last time to His Apostles on the Mount of Olives, and told them again of their mission; they looked up and a cloud received Him out of their sight. Spellbound by the glorious vision they kept their eyes heavenwards, until assured by Angels that the glorious apparition would only be repeated at the end of the world. The Apostles saddened by the departure of their Master, yet joyful over His glory and promised return, retraced their steps towards Jerusalem, and went into an upper room, which we usually call the Cenacle. This was the room in which Our Lord had celebrated the last Supper with them. Epiphanius tells us that, when the Emperor Adrian visited the destroyed city, he found that this sanctuary was the only edifice to escape the general destruction. As, however, we are told in the last verse of St. Luke's gospel that they were always in the temple, praising and blessing God, many argue that the upper room of the Acts may have been one of the many outhouses, adjacent to the temple. This view apparently better explains the scene on Pentecost day. The inspired word gives us a short description of the Church as gathered in the temple or in the Cenacle, so full of charming memories. In all there are about 120 persons, divided into three classes: the eleven Apostles, the women and chief among them Mary, the Mother of Jesus; she appears here for the last time in the gospel narrative. To make up the number of 120, we may suppose that the 72 disciples who had been formed in the school of Jesus, were also there. These groups may be considered as representing the three parts of the church—bishops, clergy, and laity. The little church was persevering with one mind in prayer; prayer will always be the most characteristic part of its functions; by prayer it prepared itself for its glorious mission. This mission had been in a particular manner entrusted to the Apostles. One of them had made himself unworthy of it and had died the death of a reprobate. Judas had to be replaced to complete the mystic number of twelve. There had been twelve Patriarchs, from whom proceeded the twelve tribes of the chosen people; it seemed just that there should be twelve spiritual Patriarchs, as apostolic fathers of a new people. The thought was natural, but who was the first to formulate it to the assembled Church? This is the first but not the last time that we shall see Peter acting as chief. Historically the most important fact, connected with the election of Matthias is the position of leadership assumed by Peter. The Acts have recorded his discourse on that occasion. He begins by explaining the terrible fate of Judas. Then he specifies the qualities required in the one, who shall take his place. The candidate must have been with them during the life of Jesus, from the baptism of John up to His Ascension; he must have been an assiduous witness of the public life of Jesus. The choice was limited; apparently there were only two such witnesses, or only two that seemed worthy of the honor—Joseph and Matthias. The lots were to decide; the voters were probably the whole assembled church. They had not then received the Holy Ghost,

and the plan adopted was not necessarily to be repeated in future elections. A devout prayer preceded
the casting of lots. The votes were favorable to Matthias,.who was thus numbered with the twelve Apostles. No other particulars have come down to us
concerning his competitor, except that on one occasion the drinking of a poisoned cup did him no harm.

Nine days had passed since the Ascension; the
tenth day was the solemn feast of Pentecost, one of
the three principal feasts of the Jews; the feasts of
Easter and of the Tabernacles were the two others.
The first Pentecost of the Christian Church fell on a
Sunday. As the Jews had gathered in Jerusalem for
the occasion from all parts of the then known world,
Jerusalem on that day was a truly cosmopolitan city.
The celebration began on the previous evening; according to Hebrew custom, the small Christian community had watched in prayer. On the morning of
the feast, while the sacrificial offering was in progress
in the temple, there came a sound as of a mighty wind
filling the whole house. The breath of God passed
on their souls and transformed them; a tongue of fire
sat upon every one of them—the symbol of divine
love, which enkindled their hearts. It is generally
believed that they received from the Holy Ghost the
gift to preach to the people around them in their own
language. Upon that supposition another question
was based; viz., whether the Apostles in reality spoke
the many different languages, or speaking one—their
own—were understood by their hearers in their own
language. Those who had received the Holy Ghost,

not only the Apostles, mingling with the crowd, were heard to speak the language of all; this does insinuate that there was no question of preaching, because this was not the office of all, and certainly not of all at the same time. The first part of the wonder must be understood rather of praying than of preaching; they heard them speak in their own tongues of the wonderful works of God. Many wonder, and others scoff, declaring that they were full of new wine. Only then the preaching begins and Peter alone is the orator; he speaks in Aramaic or in Greek, but in one language only; there is no trace in the narrative of a multiplicity of languages. In addition to the occurrence on Pentecost day, Scripture mentions other occasions, on which the gift of languages was repeated; the gift was not limited to the Apostles, but extended to the whole Christian community all through the strictly apostolic times, but in praying, not in preaching. There is no mention in the discourse of Peter of preaching in foreign tongues on his part or on the part of his companions, not even when he defends them from the charge of drunkenness, although the argument would have been most conclusive.

The above extraordinary events should not make us lose sight of the principal miracle on Pentecost—the interior transformation of the Apostles. Christ had described the descent of the Holy Ghost as the finishing touch of their moral education. The Holy Ghost was to be a light of truth to their minds, a flame of love to their hearts; He was to teach them all truth, and give them strength to perform their apostolic duties: God revealed Himself to them and through them to all others under that form of love, which grasps truth more firmly, diffuses it more liberally and makes it the law for action.

These men, rough by nature, devoid of all intellectual culture, rose through the fullness of the Spirit to the dazzling heighths of religious truth. Hesitating up to then in the truths, which they had learned, and fearful up to cowardice in professing them, they found in an unconquerable faith, an invincible courage,—the courage to defy public opinion. The Holy Ghost has come down upon the Apostles; Christ had promised that He would abide with the Church for ever; and therefore the miracle of Pentecost is in its chief purpose, immanent in the Church. The Holy Ghost, by an unseen operation, acts on the souls of the just, and produces in them enlightenment and pious impulses, always in keeping with the aspirations of the Church itself. Christ had told His Apostles that they would receive the power of the Holy Ghost coming upon them, and that they were to be witnesses unto Him in Jerusalem, and in all Judea and Samaria, and even to the uttermost parts of the earth. The first part of this message was now fulfilled; the Apostles well equipped for their work, were now to begin the fulfilment of the second part.

Pentecost was the consecration of the Church and its solemn inauguration in the world. The time had come for the Apostles to speak, not only to actuate their zeal, but also in self-defence. Peter, as supreme visible head of the infant Church, pronounced the first apology of Christianity. After an introduction throwing ridicule on the false charge of drunkenness, Peter appeals to an authority, admitted by the audience—the inspired Scriptures of the Old Testament and especially the Prophet Joel. The Jews that surround him are the same as those, who fifty-two days before, inspired by hatred, had demanded the death of Jesus. The great stumbling block for them is the death of the one, who had called Himself the Messiah. Hence the unanswerable argument of Peter is His Resurrection. The Resurrection of Christ was to His Apostles the proof of His divinity. Peter and his companions had had their faith shaken, when they saw Him in the hands of His enemies and dying on the cross. Peter understood the feelings of his audience, and was therefore well prepared to overcome their difficulties. He removes the scandal of the cross with the prophecies, which they admitted, and then preaches the Resurrection also foretold, and to which hundreds of witnesses could testify. Peter proves that Christ is the promised Messiah, but does not insist upon proving that the Messiah is God.

Christianity is not a scientific system like history or physics, which demands great intellectual attainments to arrive at a thorough knowledge of cause and effect. Acceptance of Christianity was to be an act of virtue, affecting the intellect as well as the will; it would not be an act of virtue, if conviction were based on purely syllogistic conclusions, like the working out of a mathematical problem. Peter demanded of his hearers, not learned research, but humble submission in penance and baptism. They were to believe firmly, on the strength of prophecies, of the gift of miracles which they had admired, and of the Resurrection of Christ which Peter and the others had witnessed, that the same Jesus, whom they had nailed to the cross, was by God constituted the Lord of all things, and the Christ or Messiah. They had to be converted to save themselves from this perverse generation. "They that received Peter's word were baptized." This passage of the Acts clearly insinuates human freedom in the acceptance of revelation. The grace of God and man's coöperation are both necessary for salvation. In presenting the object of faith the same facts are presented to all; these facts are sufficient to convince any one, but God will not take from man his free will; hence some receive the gift of faith, while others reject it. The second chapter of the Acts closes the narrative of the events on Pentecost day with the remark that about three thousand souls were added. Added to what? To the body of the Christians, to the Church perfectly constituted before the Apostles made their appearance in public. The new converts did not form the first community of Christians, nor a new one; they simply joined the existing Church; no compromise was effected, because faith is one and indivisible. The Church offers all it received, no more, no less.

CHAPTER FOURTH

THE RELIGIOUS LIFE OF THE FIRST CHRISTIANS

AFTER the solemn consecration of the Church on Pentecost day, and after the discourse of St. Peter about three thousand people had been converted. Shortly after that, as the Acts (IV) record, more joined; the number of the faithful was then fully five thousand. Most of these, if not all, were in all probability citizens of Jerusalem. Although some of the dispersed Jews may have been converted, and become active missionaries in their own respective towns and villages, we will not now consider them in connection with the religious life of the first Christians in Jerusalem. The converts of St. Peter had probably been the most faithful followers of Jewish traditions in the Capital. No human consideration or attraction could have brought about a conversion, which implied a severance of former ties, that might have serious material results. Only those best grounded in biblical knowledge and mystically inclined could conceive of a Messianic mission in the lowly and religious figure of Jesus. These longed after His coming and scrupulously followed the Mosaic law. There were two varieties of Pharisees at the time, of which we write— the sincere and the hypocrites. Both entertained an exaggerated religious sentiment combined with narrowness of mind; in some that feeling was sincere, in others it was a pretext for villainy. Christ repeatedly cursed the latter variety. Simon who invited Him to his table, or Nicodemus who came to Him secretly do not belong to that class. The first Christians were converts from sincere Phariseeism. After accepting the teachings of Christianity, they still preserved a great respect for the Mosaic law, because it was not yet clear that Christianity had released them from that yoke. Had not Christ Himself assured His hearers in His sermon on the Mount that He had not come to destroy the law but to perfect it? He Himself had been all through life a faithful observer of it. Such were the views of a powerful group in the infant Church. The better part of the law, that is, its moral precepts were to remain in force and the rest, rather than being suppressed, was transformed into something better. Christ had prepared His Apostles for this transition. As the dim twilight prepares our eyes for the bright rays of the sun, so does God temper the light of truth to the eye of the soul. Not to scandalize His weak contemporaries, Christ had shown Himself full of condescension for the observance of the law. Christ had announced to the Samaritan woman at the well of Sichar that the day was near, when the worship of God would not be restricted to the Temple of Jerusalem, as ordered by Moses, but be extended to the whole world. Christ had repeatedly told His followers that He had come to establish a new kingdom to be ruled by new laws. The little Church at Jerusalem, while sincerely attached to Christ, still considered itself Israelitic. This consideration enables us to understand the workings of the Primitive Church and the dissensions raised within it. Fealty to the Mosaic law manifested itself in the religious practices. The center of Mosaic worship was the temple, which Jesus had so often honored by His presence, and the destruction of which He had predicted. The Acts tell us (II.46) that they continued daily with one accord in the temple; they were regular attendants at the times prescribed by the law. We see (III.1) Peter and John going up into the temple for their morning prayer. The temple was the principal, but not the only, religious meeting place. The yearly visit to the temple did no longer satisfy the religious zeal of the Jews, especially of those outside of Jerusalem; other meeting places called synagogues were erected; in these, however, no sacrifices were offered; prayer, reading of parts of Scripture and comments on these, were the features of the service. The Talmud mentions many synagogues even in Jerusalem, notwithstanding the proximity of the temple. The synagogues were no competitors with the temple, which alone remained the center of religious worship. Our Lord during His lifetime often entered them, and there is no reason to believe that the Apostles and the disciples objected to visiting them. Many of the practices of Hebrew worship were adopted in the Christian liturgy. Externally the infant Christian Church might have been looked upon as a Jewish sect, but it was internally animated by a new spirit. The symbolism of the new faith, accepting Jesus Christ as Redeemer, found its first expression in the baptismal rite. Peter had made it plain to his hearers on Pentecost day that penance and baptism were necessary conditions for admission into the Church, of which he was the visible head. Penance came first, because without that interior disposition the external rite of baptism would not have profited; but penance without baptism, if it could be received, was similarly valueless. The baptism of Jesus, that is, the baptism instituted by Jesus, was something entirely new, not to be limited in its application to the Jews only; Christ had attributed a special efficacy to it, and gave us the ritual form of it. To the Jews was offered the first opportunity of receiving it; Peter had told them so, after showing them from Scripture their favored place in the plan of divine economy. Paul will afterwards tell them so (Eph. II.13). Peter assured the Jews on another occasion that the first fruits of the Gospel will be for them, but intimated at the same time that they shall not have the monopoly of it.

The memory of Jesus was quite fresh in the minds of the neophytes, and, needless to say, His life must have been the chief topic of their spiritual conversations; for the Apostles it was a duty to explain the details of that life. The Apostles were the authentic depositaries of dogma, and of the history of Jesus, and the faithful were persevering in the doctrine of the Apostles (Acts II.42). The moral code of the primitive Church was as plain as its teaching; Jesus was the compendium of the new faith; charity was to be the distinctive feature of its life; the faithful were of one heart and one mind.   As the number of believers increased, that perfect harmony of minds and hearts became more difficult to preserve, but it will ever remain the ideal.   The primitive Church had an individuality all its own, distinguishing it from the Synagogue both in faith and practice.   The old synagogue may be absorbed by the new Church, but can never be identified with it; there are too many radical discrepancies.   The new Church accepts Christ as Messiah and as God; the synagogue obstinately refuses to admit Him as such; God is pictured by the Jews as one particularly interested in the material welfare of His people; the God-Man of the Christians is above all solicitous for the spiritual and eternal welfare of His followers.   With the Christians God is the Father of all; with the Jews nationalism had obliterated the universal fatherhood of God.   With the synagogue religion consisted in a variety of practices; for the Christians it is summed up in the one great commandment of charity.   Grace and truth came from Jesus Christ, says St. John (I.17); truth through faith, grace through the sacramental system.

We have already mentioned baptism as the first means, whereby the grace of God was obtained, converts were added to the Church, and their sins forgiven.   The neophytes then received the Holy Ghost, as St. Peter had said in his sermon on Pentecost (Acts II.38).   Whether in the early days of the

Church the gift of the Holy Ghost was received in an extraordinary way like in the case of the Apostles, or in the ordinary way through the imposition of hands, is not quite certain. It is, however, certain that a little later (VIII) the Holy Ghost came down upon the converts of Philip at Samaria through the ministry of the Apostles, after prayer and the imposition of hands, in the ordinary way through what we now call the sacrament of Confirmation.

It is evident that what we now call the Holy Eucharist was the central part of the liturgy in the primitive Church. The Acts tell us (II.42) that the first Christians were persevering in the doctrine of the Apostles and in the communication of the breaking of bread. A little further on (II.46) we learn that the faithful continued breaking bread from house to house. In the first of these texts the Holy Eucharist is meant by the breaking of bread, because it is inserted between two strictly religious acts—the preaching of the Apostles and the liturgical prayers. St. Paul refers to it more explicitly: "And the bread we break, is it not the partaking of the Body of the Lord?" (1 Cor. X.16). The Syriac version translates the passage by the breaking of the Eucharist. In the second text the breaking of bread does probably not mean the Eucharist; the context seems to suggest the ordinary sense. These meetings from house to house, or as St. Paul writes later on to Philemon (I.2) "the Church which is in thy house" are the first signs of autonomous Christian life and emancipation from Judaism; the temple and the synagogues are not the only meeting places. The Jewish temple did not lend itself to the celebration of this new mystic rite, and besides the early Christians zealously hid the sacred mysteries from the profane eye. We may suppose that from the beginning those who had good houses placed them or parts of them at the disposal of the Apostles for the celebration of the sacred liturgy. Frequent Communion was certainly in vogue among the first Christians, and in all probability under both appearances of bread and wine, although this was not essential. Though the breaking of the Eucharistic bread only is mentioned, this does not necessarily limit Communion to the one appearance. The Eucharist must always be what it was in the beginning—a sacrament and a sacrifice of the new law. There may be a development in the ceremonial, but the substance must invariably remain the same. As the Christians met in the poor houses of Jerusalem and later on in the underground catacombs, before the splendid churches were erected, they always met at the common Eucharistic table, spread for them by Jesus Christ.

The Eucharistic rite has lost in the course of ages one of the ceremonies that accompanied its celebration in the beginning; we mean the agape or social meal. Intense brotherly love inspired the idea, but it could and did lead to abuses, as we gather from the writings of St. Paul. The spirit of charity was the moving force in the Primitive Church; it united the faithful; the glorious example attracted the best elements among those who had grown tired of strife. "The Lord increased daily together such as should be saved" (Acts II.47).

CHAPTER FIFTH

ECONOMIC ORGANIZATION OF THE PRIMITIVE CHURCH

THE dogmatic, moral, and liturgical code of the Church differentiated it from Judaism; it had begun its autonomous life, both religious and economic. The first Christians constituted truly one family; there was not only union of hearts, but also a common patrimony. The Acts clearly and repeatedly say so. "All things were common unto them, and distribution was made to every one, according as he had need" (II.32). Scripture tells us that there were no needy among them, because the owners of lands and houses sold them, and brought the price of the things they sold and laid it down before the feet of the Apostles. Two occurrences related in the Acts, as illustrating the absence of need, are of special interest to understand the economic organization of the infant Church. Among the neophytes there was a man named Barnabas of the tribe of Levi, a Cyprian by birth. He had inherited a piece of land, sold it, brought the price and laid it at the feet of the Apostles. A question suggests itself. After St. Luke stated that this was the ordinary way on the part of those neophytes, why does he single out Joseph, whom the Apostles surnamed Barnabas? It is not likely that he did so for the purpose of upholding Barnabas, as an honorable exception to the general rule, but on account of the importance of the donor in the early history of the Church, and perhaps to oppose the faithfulness of Barnabas to the deceit of Ananias and Saphira. This leads us to inquire whether this communism was obligatory or free on the part of all the members. The communism of the early Church does not necessarily run parallel with the theory advocated by many in the present day. The acceptance of that community of property was entirely free and voluntary; the custom was local and peculiar to the church of Jerusalem. From the letters of St. Paul we must conclude that it did not exist elsewhere. It was a temporary arrangement, even for Jerusalem, and it was abrogated as soon as conditions permitted. The practice, while it lasted, did not belong to the essence of a Christian life; it was a counsel then as it is to-day to give up everything and follow Christ; perhaps in the beginning that counsel was more generally followed.

An occurrence following closely upon Barnabas' generous act furnishes a clearer insight into the economic life of the first Christians. Ananias and Saphira had sold a piece of property; and retaining part of the price, they brought the balance to the Apostles under pretence that the donation represented all they had received for their property. They tried to associate exterior virtue with a sinful act—a lie; but this has never been acceptable to God. Peter said to the man: "Why hath Satan tempted thy heart, that thou shouldst lie to the Holy Ghost, and by fraud keep part of the price of the land?" (Acts V.3). Peter does not rebuke Ananias so severely for the fact that he had retained part of the price, on the contrary, he tells him that he could conscientiously have kept it all; but because he had lied to God by trying to deceive him, the supreme head of the Church. This proves that the communism of the first Christians was spontaneous and free on their part. This is further borne out by the fact that the Acts clearly state (XII.12) that Peter came to the house of Mary, the mother of Mark; the house had evidently not been sold nor deeded over to the Church. Any property owner was, after his conversion to Christianity, perfectly free to retain or sell his property; no authority could oblige him to do one or the other, and no rebuke for either was to be feared. Any one selling his property and giving the price to the Church acquired the right to being maintained by the Church. Ananias and Saphira tried to acquire that right without complying with the preliminary conditions. The cause of this communism in the Church of Jerusalem is to be found in the contempt of riches on the part of the first Christians. The teaching of Jesus had prepared them for that disregard of temporal wealth; He had called riches thorns that prevent expansion of the word of God; He had often warned His followers not to worry over food or clothing, but He did not dispense them from work; the curse pronounced upon man in the garden of Eden was not removed, but work was not to absorb the whole energy of a man created for heaven. Christ with His disciples held all in common; He apparently attached so little importance to money, that He suffered a thief to be treasurer. Perhaps also the first Christians were of the opinion that the end of the world was near. The best motive for this contempt of riches is to be found in the real brotherhood that united the first Christians; brotherhood then was not a meaningless word. True brotherhood finds or makes men equal; it opens the purse, sometimes even inconsiderately. The above causes led to this unscientific primitive communism. It was certainly not good financing to amass a social capital, without a return, to be consumed slowly but surely. The system had its imperfections; we have a proof of it in Ananias and Saphira; fraud was possible, and there is nothing to show that they were all saints. In the sixth chapter of the Acts we learn, that complaints were made by the Hellenists or Greeks, claiming that their widows were being neglected in the daily distribution. Jerusalem harbored then not only Jews born and educated in Palestine, and who read the Old Testament in Aramaic, but also Jews born and educated elsewhere and who had adopted Greek as their mother tongue; they read the sacred books in that language. We treat of Jewish converts of both varieties. They were indeed all one in faith, but the Palestine Jews considered themselves the aristocrats; they were prejudiced against the outsiders and were strong in numbers. After their conversion human frailty perdured and those who had not grown up under the shadow of the temple were somewhat neglected in the daily distribution. The widows especially, were the objects of their pious solicitude; the Mosaic law had granted them special privileges. A precious heritage that could not be neglected in the Christian Church! Abuses crept in that might have had serious consequences; the economic exceptions in favor of the Palestine Jews might eventually have developed in the religious field. Could the Church sanction such dissension? The Apostles were appealed to; they settled the dispute at once, reserving for a future occasion the right to combat Jewish pretensions, as they would appear. The blame for the unequal distribution naturally fell upon the Apostles, who up to then had retained the whole responsibility; all the functions of the infant Church were in their hands. Christ had left the organization of it to them; as needs increased, new organisms were called into existence; the work was divided.

A new need presented itself to the Apostles; the responsibility of economic administration clashed with their apostolic duties, chief of which was preaching the word of God; it placed unnecessary obstacles in the way of efficacious preaching. To offset the murmuring of the Hellenists, and to do justice to all, the Apostles ordained seven deacons, who had been selected by the people so that they might have the good will of all. The Apostles, by the imposition of their hands upon them, transmitted to them some of their powers and the grace of God to enable them to discharge their duties properly. The Apostles could then devote all their time to prayer and the ministry of the word. Judging from the names of the seven deacons we are inclined to believe that the vote was favorable to the complainants—the Hellenist portion of the flock. The more prominent of the seven were Stephen and Philip; we will have occasion to treat of these again. Of four others we know little more than their names, either from the Acts or from Christian tradition. History busied itself considerably concerning the last-named, Nicolas, a proselyte of Antioch, a Greek of non-Jewish parentage, a convert to the Jewish faith first and then to Christianity. Efforts have been made to connect him with the Nicolaites and a Gnostic sect of that name and of unsavory reputation, but it is not certain and rather improbable that a heretic should have been thus honored by the Primitive Church. The faithful designated the persons, but did not convey an authority, which they did not possess; that came directly from the Apostles. They were ordained by the Apostles for the purpose of serving tables in the daily administrations, but their work was not limited to that. They were zealous missionaries in a subordinate position; the Acts clearly tell us so of Stephen and Philip. In Scripture they are not called deacons. In another chapter we shall treat of deacons and deaconesses in the Primitive Church.

The economic organization, as explained above, was peculiar to the Church of Jerusalem; no trace of it is to be found anywhere else. In the numerous churches, which St. Paul founded, the converts kept their property and disposed of it as they pleased. The Apostle of the Gentiles ordered collections to be made, as the churches do to-day. The organization at Jerusalem apparently had not been a success; the patrimony slowly disappeared and great poverty prevailed. St. Paul had to call upon his converts to come to the relief of their brethren in Jerusalem. Yet Christian charity will always be the best solution of the social economic problem.

CHAPTER SIXTH

FIRST PERSECUTIONS OF THE CHURCH

THE Founder of the Church—Jesus Christ—had foretold to His Apostles and their followers what they were to expect from the world for their ministry and their faith. The disciple was not to be above his master nor the servant above his lord (Matt. X.24). The world despised, hated, and persecuted Christ; His followers would be treated in like manner; they would be hated by all for His sake (Matt. X.22). The connationals of the Apostles would turn them out of their synagogues and scourge them; but they were prepared by their Master to meet the attacks, that would pour down upon them on all sides. When the storm broke they were not surprised, no more than an experienced captain on a stormy sea. For the Apostles, persecution was a proof of their Master's divinity and His all-wise Providence, causing this means of destruction to extend the benefits of the Church; the blood of Martyrs will prove to be the seed of Christians. Christianity found its first recruits among the Jews; among them it found, not only cold indifference, but also open hostility. The Jews tried to smother the new religion in its infancy. We will not now examine what effect the opposition of the Jews had on the rulers of the Roman empire, but limit our remarks to the first persecutions recorded in the Acts.

A few days after Pentecost, as Peter and John were speaking to the people, the priests, the officer of the temple, and the Sadducees came upon them. They were grieved that the Apostles taught the people, and in Jesus preached the resurrection from the dead. They laid hands upon them, and held them in durance till the next day: for it was now evening (Acts IV). Peter and John were guilty of having worked an undeniable miracle in the name of Jesus of Nazareth. Immediately upon the spreading of the news, a great multitude gathered around the wonderworkers. Peter took occasion of it to address the assemblage and proclaim the divinity of Jesus Christ, by whose power and in whose name the miracle had been performed. At the time of Christ the Jews were divided into two religious factions—the Pharisees and the Sadducees. The severe rebukes, which Our Lord on various occasions administered to the Pharisees, are clear proofs of their bigotry and intolerance. They formed an active political party, whose program included hatred and war to the Romans, avoidance of all contact with them as far as possible, and their expulsion from the country, if the propitious time should ever come. There was, however, an opposition party—the Sadducees—who prompted by the spirit of contradiction took a distinctly different view of religion. The Pharisees were fanatics and anxious to impress their views upon all others; the Sadducees were indifferent, recruited chiefly among the upper strata of society, and preserved exterior respect to Mosaic practices, but without any interior spirit. The Acts (XXIII.8) tell us that one of the differences between the Pharisees and the Sadducees was the belief of the former in the resurrection of the dead, and in the existence of Angels and Spirits, which the Sadducees rejected. This explains the different treatment of the two parties at the hands of Our Lord. Christ frequently took occasion to chastise the Pharisees, and apparently did not take the same notice of the Sadducees; the Pharisees were most likely the better of the two. They took a deeper interest in religion and were more open to conviction than the Sadducees, who looked upon a materially happy life as the limit of their desires. The Sadducees did not make any efforts at proselytizing; they were a harmless element, with whom Our Lord rarely came into contact, while contact with the Pharisees was of almost daily occurrence. The bigoted fidelity of the Pharisees to Mosaic institutions grievously offended the indifference of the Sadducees. We can imagine how the religious enthusiasm of the first Christians must have been a beam in the eyes of the Sadducees. The Sadducees concluded that not only the Pharisees, but also the Christian party were opposed to them. They depended largely for their influence upon the sacerdotal class. Jesus had threatened to dry up that source of revenue and honor, by substituting to the Jewish religion and practice, a creed of which He was the chief exponent, and that promised to do away with the temple and consequently with the offerings and sacrifices. The Sadducees, seeing the ground slipping from under their feet, took advantage of the hatred of the Pharisee and the jealousy of the Roman, to combine with them in the death of Jesus. They hoped never to be troubled again about the resurrection, which they denied. But the crucified and dead Jesus of Nazareth is risen, and begins to speak again and to be spoken about. A fact so well proved by hundreds of living witnesses upsets all their calculations. The extraordinary occurrence had aroused deep interest among the Jewish people in Jerusalem. On Pentecost day three thousand gave up their previous views, and joined the small crowd of followers of the Nazarene; in a short time the number rose to five thousand not counting the women and the children. The creed of the Sadducees had received its death-blow. A retaliation on their part was to be expected; the miracle of Peter and John in favor of a lame man was the pretext for it. The Sadducees, the priests, and the officers of the temple were in the plot. They apprehended the Apostles in the evening, and held them over until morning, when they would take them before the Sanhedrim. The Apostles were in the temple; it was an easy matter to apprehend them; they offered no resistance.

The Sanhedrim was at that time the supreme religious authority among the Jews. It was composed of the high-priest, the scribes who were the experts of the law, and the ancients who were neither scribes nor priests. Annas is called in the Acts the high-priest, not because he was then, but because he had been; the position now was held by his son-in-law—Caiphas. John and Alexander, of whom we know no more, were elected to assist the Sanhedrim. The same people, who had condemned Jesus a few weeks before, caused the arrest of the Apostles. They were asked with reference to the miracle: By what power and in what name have you done this? The same question had been put to the Master. The Sanhedrim knew perfectly well in what name the Apostles had cured the lame man; they wanted their confession to implicate them. If the Apostles had been questioned two or three months before, they might have hesitated; but they are no longer the same men; they have been transformed by the Holy Ghost and now eagerly seize every opportunity to proclaim the praises of Jesus. Peter filled with the Holy Ghost again acts as speaker, and proves to his judges the divinity of Christ by the miracle. However anxious the members of the Sanhedrim were to condemn, they could not deny the supernatural fact; all Jerusalem knew that it had been performed in the name of Jesus. They discuss the question among themselves, and conclude that all they could do was to impose silence upon the Apostles. The Apostles could not submit to such a sentence, and in the spirit of true freedom of conscience, they offer a question to the judges, which they request them to answer; "Is it just in the sight of God to hear (obey) you rather than God?" It was a question very moderate and forceful at the same time; there was no escape for the judges. They could not punish them for fear of the people, because all men glorified what had been done. But the Sanhedrim insisted upon its useless threats and sent them away. The same answer will be given by all the Apostles and all their followers in all future and similar circumstances; we must obey God rather than man. If all authority comes from God there can be no true authority against God. Their conscience compelled the Apostles to speak the things, which they had seen and heard.

The Apostles had been warned and they knew that their ministry would not have a peaceful course. Judaism in all its forms challenged Christianity, and, needless to say, Christianity accepted the challenge; prayer will be its first preparation for the fight. The first persecution was bloodless; Peter and John after their recovery of freedom returned to their brethren. They had made a deep impression upon their audience; looked upon as uneducated and ignorant they argued with great wisdom. The judges could not contest their words, nor deny them, and yet they refused to believe. As an act of faith is prompted by the will, they did not believe, because their will was wickedly disposed. Upon the return of the two Apostles, the Christian community, one in heart and mind, lifted their voices to God; they saw in the occurrence nothing but an act of God's kind providence, and the fulfilment of a prophecy of the Royal Prophet: The Gentiles rage; the people meditate vain things; the kings stand up; and the princes assemble against the Lord and His Christ. The motive will be the same in all subsequent persecutions; hatred of the Christian name will cause blood to flow in streams and people heaven with martyrs. The Apostles and those with them, pray God that in the face of all dangers they may with confidence speak His word. The place was moved and through another miracle like that on Pentecost day they were strengthened in the faith. A short lull preceded the breaking out of another storm more severe than the first. The kindness and the supernatural power of the Apostles had endeared them to the common people; the opposition had to count with them; if the old law of retaliation had been kept in force, the Pharisees and the Sadducees might not have acted against the Apostles with impunity. Many signs and wonders continued to be wrought by the Apostles; fear of the Jews prevented many admirers from joining them. The number of believers—men and women—steadily increased. Peter was held in such esteem that the people thought his shadow could deliver the sick from their infirmities. The neighboring cities brought in their sick to the Apostles, who healed them all. Annas, the high-priest and the head of the Sadducees, was filled with envy, seeing the multitude falling away from his grasp. He and his followers laid their hands, not only on Peter and John, but on all the Apostles, and put them in the common prison, not for examination, but for a serious crime. With all the Apostles in prison the Church certainly was in distress. Now and in all future persecutions, Christ will show that He is faithful to His promise, and will abide with the Church to the end of time. During the night the Angel of the Lord opened the prison doors, and led the prisoners out. The Apostles were told, not to hide themselves for fear of their captors, but to go to the temple and to speak to the people the words of Christian life. Early in the morning, the Apostles fearlessly went to the temple and taught the assembled multitude. Early also the captors of the previous day went to the prison, but found the prisoners gone; the door was closed and the guards were on duty. Finding that they had been eluded, they proceeded to the temple and requested the Apostles to follow them to the courthouse. No violence was used; they had reason to fear that the people would have protected the Apostles, and stoned their persecutors. In court they were accused of having broken a command of the Sanhedrim; although forbidden to preach the new religion, they had done so, even in the temple. Peter again as the leader, together with the other Apostles, renewed a splendid profession of their faith. The Jews were cut to the heart, and they thought to put them to death. One of the members of the council—Gamaliel—a pharisee and a doctor of the law as well as the teacher of the future St. Paul, a man respected by all, requested that the accused be put forth a little while. More tolerant than the others, who were mostly Sadducees, he took the defence of the Apostles, whether merely to oppose the bloodthirstiness of the Sadducees, or from a feeling of sympathy for men that seemed so sincere in their intentions, the Bible does not state. Gamaliel in his speech to the Sanhedrists put to them the following dilemma: If the work of these men is the work of man, it will come to nought; if it is the work of God you cannot overthrow it, and if you fight it, you fight against God. It required courage to make such a plea before a crowd raging with hatred and vengeance. The defence of the Apostles is to Gamaliel a title of glory in the Christian Church for all times to come. He had also to his credit the honor of having been the teacher of St. Paul. Whether he ever changed his views to conform with those of the converted Apostle, neither the Bible nor Tradition states. A legend claims that he was baptized by Peter and John and that his body reposes in Pisa. The Talmud says of him that in his death died the glory of the law. The eloquent words of Gamaliel had the desired effect to a certain extent; there is no question any more of a death sentence, yet the excited passions of the Sadducees demanded an escape and they sentenced the Apostles to be scourged. Each of them received 39 strokes; 40 was the legal limit, but people used to straining out a gnat and swallowing a camel, reduced it to 39. The result must have been unexpected to the Sanhedrim; the prisoners, instead of cowering under the humiliation, or quailing under the torture, rejoiced and went away happy. for having been found worthy to suffer those insults for the name of their Master. They were again warned not to preach the religion of Christ, but persecution had, if possible, stimulated their zeal, and every day they ceased not in the temple, and from house to house to teach and preach Christ Jesus (Acts V.42).   The Apostles had probably given some of their blood in their scourging for the name of Jesus, but the honor of being the first to give his life for that Holy Name belongs to Stephen, one of the newly appointed deacons.   Stephen was full of grace and fortitude, and did great wonders and signs among the people.   Some of the synagogue of the Libertines attempted to argue with Stephen.   It is hard to say who these Libertines were; they were probably those, who 63 years before Christ had been led captives to Rome, and afterwards recovered their liberty, and returned to their own country.   The Libertines, Cyreneans and Alexandrians, Cilicians, and others of proconsular Asia were mostly Hellenists; Stephen, himself an Hellenist, made many converts among them.   Stephen's opponents were not able to resist the wisdom and the spirit that spoke.   Short on arguments they suborned false accusers, who were willing to declare that Stephen had spoken blasphemy against Moses and against God; they stirred up the people against him.   Stephen was led before the council.   The high-priest and the other councillors gazed upon Stephen's face, as if it had been the face of an angel.   The high-priest opened the proceedings and asked the accused: "Are these things so?"   St. Stephen explains to them in a lengthy discourse from the Scriptures familiar to them his position in the faith, which he proclaimed, and tells them that Judaism, as an established religious form, was bound to pass away. Stephen concluded his remarks with the following words: "You stiffnecked and uncircumcised in heart and ears, you always resist the Holy Ghost; as your fathers did, so do you also. Which of the prophets have not your fathers persecuted? And they have slain them who foretold of the coming of the Just One, of whom you have now been the betrayers and murderers" (Acts VII.51–52). Such language the Jews never had heard before; the doom of Stephen was now sealed. He had before him, not impartial judges, but men who were cut to the heart, and who gnashed their teeth at him. Taking him out of the city they stoned him to death. The first martyr, before returning his soul to God, falling on his knees prayed, as his Master had prayed on the cross: "Lord, lay not this sin to their charge." Under the leadership of Gamaliel, devout men, not Christians at that time, took charge of Stephen's body, which remained unburied in a field, where it had been thrown to be devoured by vultures and wild animals. They took charge of the body and made great mourning over him. Hardly seven months had passed from his ordination to deaconship to his glorious martyrdom. Saul was consenting to his death and perhaps owed his conversion to St. Stephen's prayer.

That same day a great persecution broke out against the Christians of Jerusalem. This was the first general persecution. Some think that in a short time two thousand Christians were killed. Although the exact number is unknown, we may conclude from

the testimony of St. Paul that many were killed:
"When they were put to death, I brought the sentence" (Acts XXVI.10).   Many are of the opinion
that Mary Magdalen, with her sister Martha, and her
brother Lazarus, together with Maximin, Marcella,
and Joseph of Arimathea, were put aboard of a small
craft without sails or oars, to perish at sea, but that
they eventually landed at Marseilles.   Practically all
other members of the Church, except the Apostles,
were dispersed through Judea and Samaria.   Drawing good from evil God permitted this dispersion to
send missionaries of the Christian faith to various
parts of the world; the exiles went about preaching
the word of God.   Saul was still making havoc of
the Church; entering in from house to house, and
dragging away men and women, he committed them
to prison (Acts VIII.3).

The Church had now received her baptism of
blood; her progress will be more remarkable than
before.

CHAPTER SEVENTH

AFTER the descent of the Holy Ghost on the day of Pentecost, Mary, the Mother of Jesus, disappears from the inspired writings; she was then at prayer with the Apostles, and received the Holy Ghost. We can imagine how during her stay in Jerusalem the Apostles must have been inspired and encouraged by her; she shed a benign influence on the infant Church. Mary probably remained in Jerusalem until the dispersion of the Apostles. Her adopted son—St. John—then took her with him to Ephesus. It is surprising that so little is known with any degree of certainty of Mary's sojourn in that city of Greece. The Acts, although called of the Apostles, are very reticent concerning eleven of the twelve Apostles; they are chiefly the acts of Peter and Paul. The years of their apostolate must have made history, but with chapters unknown. Their sole ambition was to extend the limits of Christ's kingdom, and to gain souls for Him, so much so that none of them left us a record of his own apostolic labors. No wonder that the Mother of Jesus shared the same fate. There is no doubt, however, that the wishes of her dying Son were carried out. She followed the loved and loving

disciple in his travels and eventually settled in
Ephesus. All we know about her life there and her
death in her native land comes from the early Christian writers. They tell us that she was apprised by
an angel of her approaching death; the day and the
hour were revealed to her. The fulfilment of God's
will was at the moment of the Incarnation, and in
every act of her life, her most earnest wish. We may
suppose that in keeping with that holy will, she
sighed after her native land and longed to die in the
shadow of Calvary. St. John, with whom her wishes
were at all times commands, made immediate preparation for returning to Palestine. After an absence of
several years, Mary returned to the land of Israel,
and took shelter in the house sanctified by the
descent of the Holy Ghost. St. John at once informed St. James, the first bishop of Jerusalem and
a cousin of the Blessed Virgin, as also the numerous
faithful in the Holy City, that the Mother of Jesus
had come to die among them. All could notice that
she had escaped the destroying action of time. St.
Denis, an eye witness of the death of the Blessed
Virgin, affirms that, at that advanced period of her
life, she was still strikingly beautiful. It is easier
to imagine than to describe the death bed scene—the
grief of the Apostles, the joy of the Mother in the
speedy reunion with her Son, her blessing to the poor
orphans, whom she was about to leave. Her soul
disengaged itself without an effort from its fair and
virginal covering, and gloriously took its flight to
heaven. It is generally admitted that the Blessed

Virgin died during the night preceding the fifteenth of August, but the year is uncertain. Some think that her death occurred eleven years after the death of Christ; others make it the year 48 of our era; some give her age at the time of death 61, others 66 years. "At the death of the Mother of Jesus," says St. Jerome, "all the host of heaven came to meet her, singing hymns and canticles which were heard by all present."

On the following day the faithful brought in with pious profusion the most precious perfumes for the burial of their Queen. They embalmed her body according to the custom of her people, but the blessed remains exhaled a sweeter odor than all the perfumes. When the time for burial had come, the Apostles carried on their shoulders the litter, in which the sacred remains had been placed, to the place of sepulture, probably in the valley of Josaphat. The faithful followed sadly and reverently. The Apostles, and especially St. John, felt their loss intensely. The sepulchral cave was closed. St. Denis, an eye witness, has left us in his "Books of divine names" his impressions of the panegyric pronounced by Hierotheus on that occasion. In praising the Blessed Virgin, the orator was almost beside himself. The Apostles had all been warned of the approaching death of the Mother of Jesus. All were present at her death and funeral, except St. Thomas. For three days the Apostles and the faithful kept up the watch at the blessed resting place, where they distinctly heard the sacred concert given by the heavenly spirits. Thomas came too late from his distant mission to be present at the death and funeral. At his request the block of stone was removed from the door of the sepulchre; he wished to take a last look at the sacred remains and sprinkle them with his tears. His request was granted, but the pure body was not there; the fresh flowers and the linen shroud was all that was left in the sepulchre. After her death heaven took body and soul, and glorified them both. After nearly 1900 years the followers of the Apostles and of the first faithful, believe just as firmly as they did, the corporal assumption of the Bl. Virgin, although it has never been declared a dogma of faith. In her liturgy the Church gave from the very beginning clearly to understand her opinion; there can be no doubt about it.

Tradition, supported by the writings of the Fathers and the religious monuments of the time, traces the devotion to the Mother of Jesus to the days of the Apostles. Peter raised an oratory in her honor in one of the ancient cities of Phœnicia; John placed a beautiful church at Lydda under the invocation of his adopted mother; Barnabas dedicated the first church in Milan to Mary. The oratory on Mount Carmel was in pre-Christian days erected in honor of the Virgin to be the Mother of God.

As the Synagogue endeavored to smother Christianity in its infancy, so it tried to stifle in the bud the devotion to the Mother of Jesus, but in vain; the

Synagogue hated the Son and despised the Mother. The Apostles therefore transplanted the veneration of Mary to the land of the stranger.

Great painters have from the beginning placed their brush at the service of the one, to whom the Greeks have given the beautiful name of Panagia— all holy. St. Luke was a painter of merit; he presented to the Cathedral at Antioch a portrait of the Virgin, painted by himself. This picture, to which God had attached signal favors, eventually came in possession of the empress at Constantinople. This is probably the painting, which the last western empress of Constantinople—Catherine of Anjou— donated to the sanctuary of Monte Vergine in Southern Italy.

In the time of St. Paul, Corinth had become a Christian city; the protecting goddess of the Corinthians was dethroned by the Panagia—the all-holy woman of the Christians.

The Apostles in the West propagated the worship of the one true God and the devotion to the Mother of Jesus. The meeting places of the first Christians were the halls and upper rooms of private houses. When these became too small, and as a further protection against spies, who then infested the empire, the catacombs were transformed into churches. Rude frescoes representing Our Saviour and His Mother, now half effaced, still proclaim the sentiments of the first Christians towards the Mother of Jesus.

Mary presided at the preparation of the Apostles

for the reception of the Holy Ghost; she communicated to the inspired writers the minute details concerning the infancy of Jesus; she encouraged the Apostles in their work as long as she lived. Favored with her Son above all mortals in her Assumption, she is now in heaven the mediatrix between God and man. Numberless volumes could have been written about the work of Christ (John. XX.25) much more could have been written about His Mother, but it was not necessary; the faith of the Christians knew then as now to worship the Son, and to honor the Mother.

CHAPTER EIGHTH

THE death of St. Stephen was the signal for a fierce persecution against the Church of Jerusalem. Saul of Tarsus made himself very conspicuous in that movement. The inspired writer of the Acts emphasizes the fact to place his conversion a few months later in bolder relief. Some months before the Jews appealed to the Romans in their hatred of Jesus; they then claimed that they were not allowed to kill any one; they had evidently overcome their scruples, when they stoned Stephen.

As the wind is one of the efficacious vehicles for the diffusion of germs, so was the wind of persecution raging in Jerusalem one of the means adopted by Providence for the propagation of the Gospel on foreign soil. While the Apostles remained in the city, the six remaining deacons very likely dispersed together with a great number of the faithful. One of them, and after St. Stephen the most prominent, crossed the border of Judea into Samaria, the province due north of Judea and south of Galilee. The chief town of the province had given it its name. The Samaritans were looked upon at that time by the orthodox Jews as schismatics. The hatred of the Pharisees was so intense that on a journey to Galilee they would make a long detour east of the Jordan, rather than follow the straight line through Samaria. No wonder that the Samaritan woman should exclaim in surprise to Christ: "How dost thou, being a Jew, ask of me to drink, who am a Samaritan woman? For the Jews do not communicate with the Samaritans" (Jno. IV.9). The friction between them was one of long standing. Several centuries before, the Assyrians had sent the Jews of Samaria into captivity, and had their places taken by people from Babylon, Cutha, Ava, Emath and Sepharvaim (4 Kings XVII.24). Those of Cutha were the most numerous. These people were pagans; they found the country infested by lions and concluded that this came as a punishment from the God of the place, whose laws they did not know. The king of Assyria, to whom they appealed in their distress, sent them a pagan priest to instruct them. From him eventually they received the Pentateuch, but they refused to accept any of the traditions of the Pharisees. When the survivors of the two southern tribes returned from their Babylonian exile, under the leadership of Zorobabel, they began at once to rebuild the temple. The Samaritans offered their services to this holy cause; but deep antipathy caused the Jews to refuse the offer. This refusal did not help to bridge over the trouble. Later on the marriage of a Jewish high-priest with a Samaritan woman, in total disregard of the traditional laws, intensified the ill-feeling. Alexander the Great permitted him to erect a temple on Mount Garizim, that would rival in splendor the temple of Jerusalem. The Samaritan woman at the well alludes to the fact in addressing Christ; "Our fathers adored on this mountain, and you say that at Jerusalem is the place, where men must adore" (Jno. IV.20). Christ had limited His ministry during His life chiefly to the Jews. "I was not sent but to the sheep that are lost of the house of Israel" (Matt. IV. 24). Israel was to be favored above all others, but St. John tells us of a real preaching of Christ to the Samaritans, and St. Luke in the parable of the ten lepers mentions the praiseworthy act of one, who returned to give thanks, and he was a Samaritan. St. Luke also relates the parable of the good Samaritan, who presents a much better figure than the Jewish priest or levite. Jesus had told His Apostles: "Go ye not in the way of the Gentiles, and into the city of the Samaritans enter ye not" (Matt. X.5). This command was only a temporary disposition, because before leaving the earth Christ said to the same Apostles: "You shall be witnesses unto me in Jerusalem, and in all Judea, and Samaria" (Acts I.8).

It was natural that Samaria on the borders of Judea should receive the good tidings before the Gentiles. The Samaritans were monotheists, and they had accepted the belief in a Messiah (Jno. IV.25). They gave proofs of their good dispositions by their willingness to receive the word of God, preached to them by Philip. Although the Bible does not give us the particular town, that was favored with his preaching, we may suppose that he selected one of the larger towns, perhaps Samaria; the appearance of Simon the Magician on the scene lends color to that opinion. Samaria was at that time a beautiful city. The Acts assure us that the people were most attentive to Philip's preaching; he confirmed his preaching with numerous miracles; the unclean spirits were driven out; many taken with palsy, and that were lame, were healed. There was great joy in the city; many men and women were baptized. One of these converts was Simon the Magician. As a magician he had seduced the people of Samaria, giving out that he was some great one. His admirers, and they were many in all walks of life, said of him: This man is the power of God, which is great. After his conversion he adhered to Philip, but as a real hypocrite. He simulated to believe in order that his followers, who had been converted by Philip, would not abandon him and also that he might receive power to speak various languages, and perform miracles, as he saw Philip and those who had been baptized by him do. He entered the Church like Judas the cenacle; the two of them are models of hypocrisy. History repeats itself and we need not wonder if there are some with us to-day. The grace of God had produced such wonderful results in Samaria, that the Apostles in Jerusalem soon heard of it. The Twelve had remained there all through the fierce persecution, either because they did not wish that flight should mean fear, or to comfort those who had remained, even if they had intended to leave the Holy City, or because they thought that Jerusalem should be the center of missionary effort. Philip in Samaria had not the fulness of spiritual powers; the Apostles had only communicated part of them to the deacons. Philip could preach, convert, and baptize, but the Apostles had to come to give to neophytes the Holy Ghost, through the imposition of hands. The Apostles selected Peter and John for that mission, which, as we have explained above, does not clash with the primacy of Peter. The Acts point out clearly that in its administration and its effects the ministry of Peter and John was something quite different from the baptismal rite, of which Christ Himself had ordained the matter and the form. Besides confirming the converts of Philip, Peter had to deal with one of them in particular—Simon the Magician. Simon wanted to buy of Peter the power to give the Holy Ghost. Peter answered him: "Keep thy money to thyself to perish with thee, because thou hast thought that the gift of God may be purchased with money" (Acts VIII.20). After this severe rebuke, Simon begs Peter's prayers that the dire calamities with which he is threatened may be averted. As we will see afterwards from church history, Simon's request was not sincere; the malice of his heart was unchanged. Being superstitious he thought the curse upon him could only be removed by the one who had called it upon his head. Our modern mediums are like the magicians of old; part of their magic, now like then, is jugglery; part of it may be ascribed to hidden biological and physical forces, and the rest to pre-ternatural agencies. The good Samaritans had not looked very closely into the magic of Simon; they simply called it the power of God. After they had confirmed the converts of Philip in Samaria, the Apostles returned to Jerusalem, and on their way evangelized many villages and hamlets. Philip remained in Samaria.

Shortly afterwards Philip was ordered by an angel to go south, and meet the eunuch of the queen of Ethiopia. He had gone up to Jerusalem on his yearly pilgrimage, and was now on his way home. Seated in his chariot, he was reading the prophet Isaiah. Philip joined him and asked whether he understood what he was reading. The eunuch admitted his inability, and wished to know to whom the passage he was reading applied. Philip explained the text to his satisfaction, and preached Jesus to him; he told him that faith in Jesus was necessary to salvation, and that the new life disposing to eternal life could only be obtained by means of Baptism. After due preparation and with the proper dispositions on the part of the eunuch, he was baptized by immersion. This does not prove that immersion is the only way to administer Baptism. It is most unlikely that the Apostles administered Baptism in this way to three thousand people on Pentecost day or in the baptism of children. After baptizing the eunuch the Spirit of the Lord took away Philip, who was found in Azotus, a place almost due west of Jerusalem. Philip then evangelized all the cities between Azotus and Cesarea, to the north-west of Jerusalem, and on the Mediterranean Sea, and he dwelled in the latter city (Acts XXI.8).

The eunuch went on his way rejoicing, and we may suppose that he became a fervent missionary in his own country. The "strangers of Rome," who witnessed the miracle on the day of Pentecost, on their return to the Eternal City, prepared the way for the Apostles; Lazarus and his exiled companions were announcing the good tidings in Southern France. Many Roman soldiers in the various provinces of the East, and on their assignment to other places very probably acted as so many missionaries. The inspired historian of the Acts is silent on all these points. He does not even tell us when precisely the Apostles dispersed to discharge the mission, imposed upon them by their divine Master. Most probably the dispersion occurred during the year following the death of Christ. Cardinal De Lai in his book on the Passion of Our Lord proves that Christ died in the year 29 of our era, not 33, as is generally believed. Before dispersing, the Apostles composed or approved what is now called the Apostles' Creed. Some think that each of them contributed one of the twelve articles; others claim that it was composed and approved by the Apostles collectively. Some think that it was composed at the meeting of the 120 persons (Acts. I.16), others fix the time after the descent of the Holy Ghost, others again in the year 44, the second year of Claudius. After the conversion of the Samaritans and of the eunuch of Ethiopia, we read no more in the inspired history about the work of most of the Apostles. James the Lesser is mentioned incidentally in connection with the Council of Jerusalem; the Acts have also a few details about the martyrdom of James the Greater. The last twenty chapters of the Acts relate the apostolic labors of Peter and Paul. For any further information about the work and death of the eleven Apostles, we depend upon the most probable Christian tradition. John wrote his Gospel on his return from exile at Patmos, where he wrote the Apocalypse. He had the supreme honor of caring for the Blessed Mother of Jesus during many years. Under the emperor Domitian he was dragged to Rome, and thrown into a caldron of boiling oil, but he came out unharmed and more vigorous than before. John outlived all the other Apostles. James the Greater, after nine or ten years of missionary labors in Judea, Samaria, and Spain, was the first of the Apostles to die a martyr's death; he was beheaded by Herod Agrippa in Jerusalem (Acts XII.2). Andrew, according to Eusebius and Origen, received Scythia and later Achaia for his mission-field; he was crucified at Patras in Greece. The priests and deacons of Achaia wrote the acts of his martyrdom, but whether they are authentic in the shape they have come down to us, is not quite certain. Philip preached in Phrygia, and was martyred at Hierapolis, being tied to a cross and stoned. Thomas preached to the Parthians, the Medes, the Persians, and even penetrated into distant India. Tradition has it that on his way out he baptized the Wise

Men—the Magi. Bartholomew went to Ethiopia and Greater Armenia; he suffered the most cruel tortures of all; with inhuman ferocity the king had him flayed alive and then beheaded. Matthew, after preaching the Gospel in Ethiopia, was put to death at the altar, pierced with a sword. James the Less was the first Bishop of Jerusalem. At the age of 96 he was stoned by the Jews and precipitated from the pinnacle of the temple. Lying half dead on the ground he begged God to forgive his executioners, and finally his head was cleft with a fuller's stick. Simon, surnamed the Zealous, worked in Egypt, Cyrene, Lybia, and other parts, and suffered martyrdom by being sawed in two. Jude, also called Thaddeus, preached in Palestine, Idumea, Syria, Mesopotamia, and Armenia, and died a glorious death by being pierced with arrows. Matthias worked in Ethiopia; tradition does not report what manner of death he died.

These eleven Apostles all died martyrs, except St. John; who underwent the tortures of a martyr, but was saved by a miracle. Few of these Apostles had a permanent see, like St. James who held the see of Jerusalem. Most of the bishoprics they founded eventually fell into the hands of heathens, and are now only titular sees; they are now given to bishops, but they have ceased to be dioceses.

Of the twelve Apostles two wrote Gospels—Matthew and John. John also wrote three canonical letters and the Apocalypse or Book of Revelations. Peter left us two letters, Jude one, and James the Less one. Seven of them did not leave us a line. All of them preached the Gospel without having a copy of the New Testament, as we have it; because St. John wrote his inspired writings after all his co-Apostles had gone to their eternal reward.

CHAPTER NINTH

CONVERSION OF ST. PAUL AND HIS CALL
TO THE APOSTOLATE

THE Acts, our sure guide in the early history of the Church and of Christianity, oppose to the peaceful and salutary work of Philip among the Samaritans, the hostile efforts of Saul. He was as yet breathing out threatenings and slaughter against the disciples of the Lord (Acts XI.1). The last time we heard of him was in connection with Stephen's martyrdom. On that occasion the witnesses laid down their garments at the feet of a young man, whose name was Saul (Acts VII.57). Saul now had no stronger desire than to kill the followers of the Nazarene. He seems to glory in the fact that he was a native of Tarsus, no mean city, as he calls it (Acts XXI.39). Indeed it was the capital of Cilicia, one of the 35 provinces, of which the Roman empire was then composed. Ancient pagan writers gave it the preference over Athens and Alexandria. This may be exaggerated, but it cannot be denied that Tarsus provided great educators to the imperial house. Probably Tarsus also surpassed in wickedness the other cities of the Greco-Roman empire. Strabo tells us that the gates of the city carried in Assyrian the following inscription, eloquent in its briefness: "Eat—drink—and be merry—the rest is nothing." Its wealth perhaps enabled the citizens to put that motto into practice, Saul bought at a great price the title of Roman citizenship (Acts XXII.28). Tarsus was a free town without the burdens of a Roman garrison, and was governed by its own laws; its citizens were not Roman citizens by birth. Saul will revindicate in the future the rights, which Roman citizenship conferred.

Saul was of the stock of Israel, of the tribe of Benjamin, a Hebrew of the Hebrews, and a Pharisee (Phil. III.5). In keeping with the Mosaic Law, he had been circumcised the eighth day and given the name of Saul in memory of their first king. He received his primary education in his native city. In connection with the synagogue there was a school, in which the hope of the future, as all children are, received his religious training; he learned to read the Scriptures. In his letter to Timothy he alludes to the profitableness of reading the Scriptures in infancy (2 Tim. III.15–17). Probably he acquired also some Greek culture in his native city. The Hebrew youth in those days were also taught a trade to provide for their subsistence. Saul became a tentmaker. We will find him working at his trade, even after he became an Apostle, in order not to be a burden to others. Saul completed his education in Jerusalem, as he himself tells us: "I am a Jew, born at Tarsus in Cilicia, but brought up in this city" (Acts XXII. 3). He had a married sister in Jerusalem (Acts XXIII.16) and perhaps he made his home with her.

His ambition probably was to be a rabbi, because he received his instruction in the law at the feet of Camaliel, one of the seven great doctors of the law. Gamaliel did more than simply prepare Saul in rabbinical dialectics, he insisted upon combining practice with theory. His teaching must have corresponded with the noble aspirations of Saul; he was above the little pedantry of the Pharisees. Saul did not imbibe the moderation of his master; animated as he was with deep intolerance he did not applaud the moderation displayed by Gamaliel, when defending the Apostles before the Sanhedrim against the Sadducees.

Saul was most probably in Jerusalem during the lifetime of Christ. At the time of the martyrdom of St. Stephen, Saul is described as a young man (Acts VII.57) probably between 20 and 40 years of age. He may have seen Jesus; if he did, the sight did not make a lasting impression upon him, no more than did His passion, death, and resurrection, of which he undoubtedly heard. He continued to make havoc of the Church, entering in from house to house, and dragging away men and women, committed them to prison (Acts VIII.3). The field of his nefarious work in Jerusalem was too limited, and therefore he asked of the High Priest letters to Damascus, to the synagogues: that if he found any men and women of this way, he might bring them bound to Jerusalem (Acts IX.2). His desire was to extinguish the Christian religion everywhere. Damascus was at that time a city of about 50,000 inhabitants. It had fallen recently into the hands of a petty king, named Aretas, a creature of Caligula. Aretas was the father-in-law of Herod Agrippa, who repudiated his lawful wife, to contract an adulterous union with Herodias, the wife of his brother. Aretas had left to the Jews their autonomy in Damascus; they could regulate themselves according to their own laws. This explains why Saul should have asked for letters to Damascus; the synagogues there although independent of those in Jerusalem, insisted upon such letters of introduction. His feelings on the way to Damascus are reproduced in some of his epistles; in his own words he was then a blasphemer, and a persecutor, and contumelious (1 Tim. I.13). His mad rage against innocent victims caused him to disregard all obstacles, but, as he afterwards confessed, it was the effect of ignorance in unbelief. Blinded by hatred for the Christian name, he rode along the road to Damascus, accompanied by men of the same frame of mind. When he drew nigh to the city suddenly a light from heaven shone round about him; he fell to the ground and heard a voice saying to him: "Saul, Saul, why persecutest thou me? Saul asked: Who art thou, Lord? The mysterious voice answered: I am Jesus, whom thou persecutest. It is hard for thee to kick against the goad" (Acts IX).

In Scripture we have three accounts of the conversion of Saul; one in the words of St. Luke (IX) and two in the words of the convert himself, the first in a discourse to the people at Jerusalem (XXII), the other before king Agrippa (XXVI) with a few extra

details, making the whole all the more attractive.
Saul did not resist the sweet invitation of Jesus;
Christ is the head of the Church, by persecuting His
followers Saul persecuted Jesus. He sought to kill
Jesus, when Jesus sought him to live. Why should
he persecute Jesus, his best friend, who had never
offended him in any way, and who at the same time
showered His blessings upon him? After that, who
could ever despair when he contemplates Saul, full of
hatred and envy, cured in a moment by the heavenly
physician? The grace of conversion was given him,
he coöperated, and therefore he will be able to say
afterwards: "By the grace of God I am what I am."
Saul had been goaded on by grace; as disregard for
whip or stick would bring to the plowing ox a more
severe application of it, so would Saul's rage and
hatred have brought dire disaster upon him. He
justly claims ignorance for his ways; it lessened his
guilt in the eyes of God, but it was not blameless,
because he could have easily overcome it.

Saul, trembling and astonished, said: "Lord, what
wilt thou have me do?" The question was prompted
by his own free will; he consented freely to the motion
of divine grace. He confesses afterwards (XXVI.19)
that he was not incredulous to the heavenly vision,
showing that he could have resisted and was not compelled to submit. The divine answer to his question
was: "Arise and go into the city, and there it shall
be told thee what thou must do." Saul will be called
directly by Christ to the Apostolate and be instructed
by Him, but as a preliminary measure God wills that

men shall be saved through the ministry of others—a doctrine, which Paul will often reiterate in his epistles. The men in company with him were amazed, having indeed heard a voice, but seeing no man. Saul arose from the ground, but opening his eyes he saw nothing. His companions leading him by the hand brought him to Damascus. For three days he was blind, and abstained from all food and drink. A follower of Christ, by the name of Ananias, and on whom great praise is bestowed in the Acts (XXII.12), was ordered in a vision to seek Saul of Tarsus in the house of Judas on Strait Street. Ananias knew Saul by reputation, and expressed his fear for approaching a man, who had come to kill all Christ's followers, if he could. The Lord reassured him and told him how Saul was a vessel of election, how great he would be as an apostle; furthermore he was now praying and changed into a new man. Ananias went on his way and found as the Lord had told him. Immediately the scales fell from Saul's eyes, he recovered his sight, was baptized, and was filled with the Holy Ghost. Ananias was according to tradition one of the seventy-two disciples. He died a martyr for the faith.

Saul was no idiot, and the vision was no hallucination. He was sure that he had seen Jesus, learned many things from Him and was appointed by Him an Apostle exactly like the other Twelve. Saul's conversion was under the influence of grace a psychological transformation. The sudden change was caused by the vision of the living Jesus; it upset his previous views immediately; the consciousness of it gave him all through life a wonderful energy in his varied and laborious apostolate. The death of Jesus was the great scandal of the Pharisaical Jew; in his eyes a man treated like Christ was, could not be the Messiah. Saul argued: "Christ was killed, but He is not dead, He lives, He appeared to me; the ignominy of the cross is transformed into the triumph of the resurrection." The scales had fallen from his eyes, and also from his mind; all his objections were solved; the risen Christ is the proof of Christianity. The same Saul will afterwards write to the Corinthians: "If Christ be not risen again, then is our preaching vain, and your faith is also vain" (1 Cor. XV.14).

The space devoted in the inspired Acts to the conversion of Saul shows sufficiently that it is a very important fact in the history of the Primitive Church, not only because he was destined to be the Apostle of the Gentiles, but because his conversion is the model of all conversions. It means the grace of God as an initial step moving both the intellect and the will, yet so that man must coöperate, and be disposed like Saul to do the bidding of God. That grace is given to all; it enlightens all men, but all do not respond.

Historians do not all agree as to the year of this wonderful conversion, whether the year following or two years after the death of Christ; the first opinion seems the more probable. Most likely the cruel persecution of the Christians, following upon the death of St. Stephen, encouraged Saul in his nefarious work, and he at once devised new means of persecuting the Church; the trip to Damascus followed shortly after. He is supposed to have been then 34 years old, and to have spent an equal number of years in the apostolate.

After his conversion Saul remained with the disciples at Damascus for a few days. During the three days of his physical blindness he was instructed by Christ Himself, and received infused knowledge and understanding of the Scriptures. Immediately after that he began to argue with the most learned among the Jews and to convince them with his arguments. All, Jews and Gentiles, and even Christians wondered over the sudden change; they could hardly believe their ears and their eyes. Was this the young man breathing out threatenings and slaughter? Saul kept on gaining in strength and confounding the Jews.

Saul did not require a special commission from the Apostles in Jerusalem, because he had received the necessary power from Christ Himself.

Scripture does not state how long Saul remained in Damascus. When he left the city he proceeded to Arabia, probably not to preach, but to prepare himself in solitude for the arduous work that awaited him. How long his retreat there lasted is unknown to us, perhaps three years, because as he himself wrote to the Galatians (I.18) after three years he went to Jerusalem via Damascus to see Peter. He did not tarry long in Damascus on his return from Arabia. The Jews consulted together; they were lying in wait for him; they watched the gates of the city day and night with the intention of killing him. The disciples let him down in a basket over the wall, and he started for Jerusalem. His sole purpose was to see Peter. Why Peter, and not James, who was then Bishop of Jerusalem? He tarried with Peter fifteen days. The Christians in the Holy City apparently had not heard of Saul's conversion; they had their misgivings about the new arrival; they feared the man, whom they knew as a cruel persecutor. Saul needed an introduction and a certificate of good behavior. Barnabas, the Cyprian born Levite, was greatly respected by the Christian community in Jerusalem. He was one of the first converts; he had sold his land and brought the price of it to the Apostles (Acts IV.36). He was also intimately acquainted with Saul, whom he had known from infancy and with whom he had frequented the school of Gamaliel. We may suppose that Barnabas tried on previous occasions to melt the hardened heart of Saul. He introduced him to the Apostles and to the Christian community. He told them what had happened near and at Damascus, how he had been called a vessel of election and had been appointed an Apostle by Christ Himself. Saul was admitted and freely moved about among them. What transpired between Peter and Saul, Scripture does not say, but it does state that Saul spoke to the Gentiles and disputed with the Greeks (Acts IX.29). We notice here an apparent contradiction. It is not likely that the converts from Judaism in Jerusalem would have suffered Saul to preach to the Gentiles, when they found fault with Peter for that reason (XI). Peter was the first to receive the Gentiles in the person of Cornelius, by command of God. How can we reconcile that with the preaching of Saul? Who were these Gentiles and Greeks? Perhaps Jews of Greece, born and educated among the Gentiles, or Greek speaking Jews; Greek was then almost synonymous with Gentile. Perhaps Paul argued with them, but did not convert them, or these Greeks may have been converts to Judaism, to whose conversion to Christianity the brethren could not have objected. If really true Gentiles are meant, then this event must have taken place after the conversion of Cornelius. St. Luke first gives us the facts illustrating the beginning of Paul's apostolate, before he relates Peter's work among the Gentiles.

Peter and Saul now know each other, they will meet again and crown their apostolic career with a glorious martyrdom on the same day of the same year in the same city. During his stay in Jerusalem Saul probably argued in the synagogue of the Cilicians, who had stoned Stephen and now sought to kill him, as a traitor and a deserter. God warned him in a vision in the temple to make haste and get quickly out of Jerusalem, because they would not receive his testimony concerning him (XXII.17–18). Saul fled not for fear, the intrepid warrior knew no fear, but because God called him to a broader field. He went to Cesarea and thence to Tarsus, the capital of Cilicia and his native city.

After that the Church had a breathing spell; peace prevailed throughout all Judea, and Galilee and Samaria; and the faithful increased in number and merits.

CHAPTER TENTH

PETER remained in Jerusalem during the spiritual upheaval following upon the death of St. Stephen, to protect the Church in the throes of the storm; the Holy City was then the mother of all other churches. But Christ had committed to him the care of the whole flock—sheep and lambs. He availed himself of the peace that followed the dreadful storm, to visit all the Christian communities, scattered in various parts of Palestine. On his tour he came to Lydda, not far from the Mediterranean and a day's journey from Jerusalem. At Lydda Peter performed a miracle on a man who for eight years had been suffering from the palsy. The sight of the miracle effected the conversion of the greatest number of the inhabitants of Lydda and Saron. Saron is the name of the great plain along the Mediterranean from Joppe in the south to Cesarea in the north; Lydda was a town in the plains of Saron. The disciples of Joppe, having heard of Peter's presence in Lydda, sent messengers to him with the urgent request for a speedy visit to their town. Peter went with them to Joppe, the present Jaffa, also on the sea, and now the starting point of the up-to-date Jaffe-Jerusalem

railway.   Joppe is the town from which Jonas started
to flee from the anger of the Lord (Jon. I.3).   A
sad sight greeted him on his arrival.   One of the
good women named Tabitha had died; the whole
community mourned the loss of their best friend.
Tabitha had been surnamed Dorcas-deer—so prompt
had she been in all works of mercy.   Peter was led
into an upper chamber; saddened widows awaited
his arrival and showed him the coats and garments
which Dorcas had made for them.   Tabitha is no
more; Peter is in presence of the mortal remains.
After all had been put out of the room, Peter knelt
down and prayed, and then turning to the body he
said: "Tabitha, arise!"   She opened her eyes and
sat up; Peter gave her his hand and lifted her up.   He
called in the saints and the widows and presented her
alive.   Many conversions were the result of this
miracle (Acts IX.39).

A more important event in the history of the
Church occurred at that time, when Peter was stay-
ing with the tanner at Joppe.   Two persons of quite
different stations in life, the one at Joppe, the other
at Cesarea—Peter and Cornelius—had a vision; the
two visions explained each other.   The Church so far
is the church of Jews, not of Gentiles; it was not yet
entirely emancipated from Judaism.   For the proper
understanding of the two visions we must first consider the latter in time.   Peter had gone up to the
roof of the tanner's house to pray; it was about noon
and he began to feel the pangs of hunger.   Whilst
dinner was being prepared, he was wrapped in ecstasy

(X.9–48).   He saw a linen sheet let down by the four corners from heaven to the earth.   In the concave surface of the sheet he saw all kinds of quadrupeds, and creeping things, and birds.   A voice said to him: Arise; (he was probably on his knees in prayer) kill, and eat.   Peter was horrified; was not disposed to eat anything unclean or common.   The voice rebuked him for calling unclean what God had cleansed. This was repeated three times and the sheet disappeared.   Peter could not make out what it meant, but soon he had an easy key to the enigma.

Cornelius was a centurion of the Italian band at Cesarea; he was not only a Roman, but his name seems to indicate that he belonged to one of the prominent families.   The inspired writer of the Acts tells us (X.2) that he was a religious man and fearing God with all his house, liberal in almsgiving and assiduous in prayer.   He had a very clear vision.   An angel appeared to him and called him by his name. Cornelius was seized with fear and whispered: "What is it, Lord?"   The angel told him that his prayers and his alms had ascended for a memorial to God, and that he should send messengers to Peter, whose address was minutely given, to call him to Cesarea; he would tell him what to do.   After the angel had left, Cornelius called two of his servants and one of his soldiers, related his vision, and sent them without delay to Joppe.   When they drew near to the city the next day, Peter had his vision.   When it had disappeared, the messengers from Cesarea stood at the gate, and asked for Simon, who is surnamed Peter. At the same time the Spirit told Peter, who was thinking over his vision, that three men wished to see him and that he should go with them, without any fear because God had sent them. Peter went out to meet the messengers, invited them in to stay overnight in the house of the tanner. The next day accompanied by some of his Jewish converts Peter started for Cesarea. It was a journey of a day and a half. Cornelius with his kinsmen and his special friends awaited Peter's arrival; all of them were most likely pagans. Cornelius went out to meet Peter, and falling at his feet, adored. Peter objected to this mark of veneration. He tells the audience at once that his views are no longer those of a real Jew; it was not any more to him an abominable act to keep company with those of another nation. When Cornelius had explained his vision, the meaning of Peter's own vision became quite clear to him. In a few chosen words Peter prepared Cornelius and those with him for their reception into the Church; he told them that God is not a respecter of persons. We cannot admit that Peter had made a new discovery of something unheard of. Christ had commissioned him and the other Apostles to preach the gospel to every creature, and to teach all nations, but either they had not fully understood the command, or they did not well know how to go about evangelizing the heathens. While Peter was speaking to his pagan audience, the Holy Ghost came down upon them and renewed to some extent the miracle of Pentecost. The Jewish converts from Joppe, who had accompanied Peter to

Cesarea, were astonished when they saw that the grace of the Holy Ghost was poured out on the Gentiles also. They had received the baptism of the Holy Ghost; Peter now commanded that they be baptized with water in the name of the Lord Jesus Christ, and they, like the three thousand on the day of Pentecost were added to the Church; no separate church was founded for the converted Gentiles. Peter's act in receiving them without circumcision meant that the very basis of the Mosaic Law had been removed. What was not necessary for converts from paganism could not be imposed upon the converts from Judaism, because the religion of Christ was the same for all, and the necessary means of salvation were the same for all.

Notice of the great event at Cesarea soon spread to Jerusalem, and the faithful there were much excited over it. After hearing what had happened, they still contended that the law was binding on all of Jewish descent, and free to the Gentiles. Peter on his return to Jerusalem was requested to explain his act; his explanation was accepted by all; "they held their peace and glorified God" (XI.18). That settled the question in so far as the admission of Gentiles into the Church was concerned. The abolition of the law for the Jews was reserved for a future occasion; the Council of Jerusalem will remove all ambiguity about that.

Paul boasted repeatedly of being the Apostle of the Gentiles (Gal. II.7) as Peter was of the Jews. Peter opened the way to the heathens in the baptism without circumcision of the first converts at Cesarea; how can Paul claim as he does? Paul never pretended that the conversion of the heathens was exclusively entrusted to him; he knew too well that the other Apostles had pagan countries assigned to their missionary zeal. If Peter was the exclusive Apostle of the circumcision, Paul invaded his field, because, as we learn from his own epistles, he busied himself also with the conversion of the Jews. Paul's boast simply means that his long and laborious apostolate was chiefly devoted to the Gentiles. There is nothing in the epistles of St. Paul to rob Peter of the honor of having received the first heathens into the Church. In his letter to the Galatians about twenty years after his conversion Paul indeed complains of opposition to his work. Did that opposition come from the Church in Jerusalem? No; he clearly says that it came from false brethren, who, like Simon the Magician, had managed to get into the fold. The true members of the Church had previously on hearing of his work, glorified God in him (Gal. I.24).

CHAPTER ELEVENTH

ELUCIDATION OF TWO IMPORTANT POINTS

One of the hardest points to settle concerning the early history of the Church is the exact date of the important events recorded in the inspired Acts and in ecclesiastical history. Cardinal De Lai has rendered a great service by proving satisfactorily, in his recent book "The Passion of Our Lord," that our Christian era antedates by a few years the birth of the Saviour. He proves that Christ died at the age of 33, in the year 29 of our era. His conclusive arguments are the following: First, Tertullian, St. Augustin, and Lactantius affirm without any hesitancy that Jesus died during the consulate in Rome of the Gemini (Twins). One of the customary methods in vogue in the Republic and later in the Roman Empire, and adopted by Latin historians, to compute time was to indicate the consuls of the year. That these names might not be forgotten, they were chiselled on marble exposed to public view. In the excavations of the Roman Forum were found marble tablets, imbedded in the walls of the basilica of Castor and Pollux, and of the palace of Numa on the Via Sacra. These tablets contained the names of the consuls. These constitute the famous Capitol records. It is at present admitted by all and beyond question that the consulate of the Gemini coincide with the first year of the 202 Olympiad, which is precisely the year 29 of the Christian era. It would be rash to question the authority of the above three writers on a date of such importance.

Another proof is the date of Herod's death. Herod died in March three years before the Christian era. This is confirmed by many conclusive arguments and above all by the great Jewish historian—Josephus Flavius. If Herod died three years before the Christian era, then it is evident that Christ was born at least four years before it, in order to explain Christ's birth, the adoration of the Magi, the presentation in the temple, the flight into Egypt, and the slaughter of the Innocents. We must then place the birth of Christ at least four years before our era, to enable us to believe, as the Bible assures us, that He was born in the days of King Herod. Up to the sixth century the great events were not dated from the birth of Christ; each nation had its own method of cataloguing events. The Hebrews counted their years from the creation of the world, or from the Patriarchs, and with marked differences, as we gather from the Hebrew and Samaritan text of the Bible, and from the version of the Septuagint. Subsequently the Hebrews passed under the dominion of the Persians, then of the Greeks, and finally of the Romans. Among the Greeks the best known date was that of the Olympiads, organized in the year 776 before the Christian era. Each Olympiad numbered four ordi-

nary years; all Greece then took part in the great
games at Olympia. The Greeks had besides their
fixed dates for great battles, the dates of the Macedons
and of Alexander the Great. Rome had its dates:
first of all that of the foundation of Rome, which according to Varro and other authorities must be put
down in the year 754 before Christ; Cato, Titus
Livius, and others put it down one or two years
nearer. Then there were the consular dates, to which
we have already alluded. Later on came the dates
of the battles of Actium, of Julius Cæsar, of Augustus, of the martyrs under Diocletian, etc. In all the
above computations the beginning of a year is most
uncertain; among the Romans themselves there were
differences concerning it.

This explains how exceedingly difficult it is to fix
with certainty the date of an event in ancient chronology.

Dennis the Little in the sixth century introduced
his system of computing time from the birth of
Christ. It was a workable system easily adopted for
common use, but elaborated without sufficient con-
trol. Dennis made mistakes and no wonder! he had
not at his disposal during the barbaric invasions of
his time all the elements, which we now have. Char-
lemagne carried this system into France, and it slowly
extended to the whole Christian world without correction. Under all the foregoing difficulties a difference of only four years is a small matter, but it is well
to know it.

The readers of the early history of the Church will

realize that it is impossible to give with absolute certainty the dates of some great events during the lifetime of the Apostles in the first century.

Another very important point in the history of the Primitive Church is its hierarchy. Peter was, as we have explained in Chapter Second, appointed by Christ to be the visible head of the church. Others were appointed by Christ to share part of his responsibility. Christ's mission was directly entrusted by Him to Peter and the other Apostles, but they were to have their lawful successors for the conversion of the world and its spiritual government. The highest authority we have concerning the Primitive Church is the inspired Acts. The superficial reader may not find in them the different grades of the hierarchy.

It is of faith however that bishops are superior to priests in both order and jurisdiction; it is theologically certain that this superiority is of divine right. With regard to Order we know from Scripture that only bishops ordained priests. The Apostles ordained priests in every church (Acts XIV.22). Titus was left in Crete to ordain priests in every city (Titus I.5). Timothy was warned not to impose hands lightly on any man (Tim. V.22). Both Titus and Timothy were bishops. With regard to jurisdiction, St. Paul tells us (Tim. V.19) that Timothy had power to receive accusations against priests and therefore to examine and punish them; only a superior can do this. Many of the early Fathers assure us that in a way the bishops may be called the successors of the

Apostles, and the priests of the seventy-two disciples;
the Apostles certainly were above the disciples.

The authority and excellence of the bishops over
the priests cannot be argued from the mere difference
of the names, as they occur in the Acts—*episcopus*
(bishop) and *presbyter* (priest or elder) and the
corresponding words in the original Greek. The
word *episcopus* (bishop) etymologically means "in-
spector" and denotes dignity and authority, but not
the nature or the grade of it. With pagan writers
the word meant a civil or military prefect. So does
Eusebius apply the term to emperor Constantine. In
the New Testament the term is constantly used to
express a spiritual inspectorship over all other Orders.
The word *presbyter* (priest) etymologically means
an elder in years, and implicitly a certain authority
that was often given to old men, but it does not express the nature of that authority, whether spiritual
or not, nor the grade. So does St. Peter use the word
when he says: "Ye young men be subject to the
ancients (presbyters)" (I Pet. V.5). So also in the
gospel of St. Matthew (XV.2): "Why do thy disciples transgress the tradition of the ancients?" Here
again in the Greek text the word *presbyter* is used to
denote the elders, doctors of the law and of tradition.

From time immemorial *bishop* designates a priest
of the first order who has power to administer Confirmation and Holy Orders; *presbyter* a priest of the
second order, who is subject to a bishop.

There is this difference between apostles and bishops that the apostles had jurisdiction and authority everywhere, whereas the bishops had theirs restricted to a certain church or territory. The charges of St. Paul to Titus and Timothy prove that he had appointed them to rule over the priests. In the Apocalypse (Ch. II.III) St. John administers a severe rebuke to the seven angels or bishops of seven churches. It is historically proved that some of them had several priests. In the letters of St. Ignatius, who died a martyr in 107, we read the following expressions: "Obey your bishop as Christ obeyed His Father, and your priests as the Apostles; honor the deacons as the law of God, that all may end in the love of God. And whereas the bishops take the place of Jesus Christ and the priests the place of the Apostles, be subject to the bishops as to Jesus Christ, and to the priests as to the Apostles; so have the Apostles themselves commanded."

If that difference had not existed, how could the Fathers of the Church in their controversy with the heretics of their time in the second and third centuries have left us a list of the bishops of the principal churches dating back to the Apostles themselves.

In the beginning the word "presbyter" applied to bishops and priests alike; they were probably all elderly men; hence in several passages of Holy Scripture the word variously designates the one or the other. St. John calls himself a presbyter (2 Jno. I.1– 3 Jno. I.1). St Peter calls himself a co-presbyter (1 Pet. V.1). When St. Paul writes of the imposition of the hands of the priesthood (1 Tim. IV.14) he seems to indicate the college of bishops and priests, who were then in Ephesus. The real question to solve is whether the word "bishop" in the New Testament invariably applies to priests of the first order, or also to presbyters-priests. Often in Scripture mention is made of bishops and deacons; it would seem at first sight that, if the presbyters constituted a separate order, they could not have been overlooked.

Some think that wherever the word bishop occurs, it always applies to a priest of the first order, and that such bishop is also presbyter, both on account of age, and of the priesthood, which he holds in a more eminent degree. In his letter to the Philippians (I.1) Paul greets the bishops, in the plural; this leads some to think that the city of Philippi may have had more than one bishop, or that the bishops of neighboring cities had met there. They also concede that in the beginning of the Church most of the presbyters were bishops.

Others take a contrary view and see in the bishops so-called in the New Testament only priests of the second order; this view does not do away with the distinction between bishops and priests. The name of apostle was often applied to priests of the first order, as in the case of Timothy, Titus, Epaphroditus, Barnabas, and perhaps Andronicus and Junias.

A more common opinion is that the appellation "bishop" in the Primitive Church was applied to priests of both the first and the second order, but that the orders were not the same, and that those of the first order excelled the others in power and jurisdiction.

The name *bishop* denotes properly the charge or the office, and applied generally to those who presided at the meetings of the Christians. In this sense the name might be applied promiscuously to priests of the first or of the second order. When St. Paul treats of those whom the Holy Ghost has placed to rule the Church of God (Acts XX.28) he designates priests of the first order. When he mentions the ancients of the church (XX.17) he includes the priests of both orders. Although Paul certainly was a bishop, he sometimes calls himself a minister (deacon) (1 Cor. III.5; 2 Cor. III.6).

Scripture demands superior qualifications from the bishops and imposes different charges upon both Orders.

The bishops ruled a church and had to promote its purity in doctrine and morals. Teaching was more especially entrusted to them. It was their duty to confirm, to ordain, and consecrate the other ministers. Priests of the second order presided over the flock assigned to them by the bishop; they administered the sacraments, except Holy Orders and Confirmation.

Mention is also made in the Acts of deacons and deaconesses. Deacon or the corresponding Greek word *diakonos* means a server, as in Matthew XX.26. More especially the word is applied to a server at table. It also signifies a sacred minister, who has a religious charge of any order, as when St. Paul says: "Let us exhibit ourselves as the ministers [deacons] of God" (2 Cor. VI.4). In a narrower sense it indicates a minister of a particular Order, who through an exterior rite is put in charge of a religious office. In that sense it applies also to deaconesses in the Primitive Church.

In the strict sense deacons are those, who through a sacramental ordination at the hands of a bishop, are consecrated for the divine ministry in the church. This Order is inferior to that of the priesthood. Scripture treats of these deacons in several places. They were the men selected in the (Acts 1.6) and mentioned by St. Paul in his letter to Timothy (1 Tim. III.8) where he enumerates the qualities and virtues required of them. The chief duties of the deacons were to minister at the altar, to baptize, and to preach. In the Primitive Church they brought Holy communion to the sick, visited the prisoners, distributed alms to the poor, etc. The first seven deacons, of whom we read in the Acts (VI.1–6) were deacons in the strict sense of the word; they were not merely for the men what the deaconesses were for the women. The deacons received the sacrament of Holy Orders. It is of faith that the hierarchy instituted by Christ consists of Bishops, Priests and at least Deacons. The hierarchy of Orders being a divine institution did exist in the Primitive Church. The following arguments prove that the seven deacons, of whom the Acts treat, were really ordained according to Christ's institution. 1. The Apostles imposed their hands with prayer, exactly as in the ordination and consecration of priests and bishops. 2. Among the virtues required of deacons are mentioned the fulness of the Holy Ghost, wisdom, etc.; these certainly were not required for profane functions. 3. After their ordination these ministers exercised their sacred functions; Stephen preached, Philip baptized, etc. 4. Whenever St. Paul writes about deacons, he does so always in connection with the bishops, and he demands great perfection and holiness in them. 5. Those of the Holy Fathers who were nearest to the apostles openly attest that the deacons were consecrated ministers; the deacons of their days were the successors of those appointed by the Apostles.

The deacons must be considered as sacred ministers, although St. Luke does not openly say so. He simply points out the occasion, on which the Apostles did as Christ had commanded them. The service of the table, especially for the widows and the poor, was simply the occasion of the institution. It does not denote the whole and exclusive charge.

Somewhat similar to the order of deacons was the institution of deaconesses. This was a mere lay organization and that is the essential difference between the two. The New Testament often mentions pious women, who in various ways helped the preachers of the Gospel. In the lifetime of Our Lord some pious women ministered unto Him of their substance (Luke VIII.2–3). Some of them followed the Apostles to take care of their material wants (1 Cor. IX.5). Other pious women were selected to look after the Christian women, and help them in all things appertaining to religion.   In the early ages of Christianity they were called deaconesses. Their duties were: 1. To be present when bishops or priests administered baptism by immersion to women; 2. To instruct privately catechumens in Christian doctrine; 3. To visit sick women and prisoners of their sex; 4. To act as janitresses in church, to assign to the women their places, and to take charge of the arrangements within for the women, as the deacons had it for the men; 5. To distribute the alms of the Church to widows and poor women.   St. Paul gives the qualities required of the deaconesses; they had to be chaste, not slanderers, but sober and faithful in all things (1 Tim. III.11).   The organization of deaconesses had entirely disappeared in the west before the end of the eighth century; it lasted longer in the Oriental Church.

CHAPTER TWELFTH

THE WRITTEN AND THE UNWRITTEN WORD

The Apostles had been appointed the messengers of the good tidings to all men in all parts of the world. What were the means employed by them for the propagation of the Christian religion?

The ordinary and principal means chosen by Christ for that purpose was the oral preaching of the Apostles and their successors. "He gave some Apostles, and some Prophets, and some other evangelists and other some pastors and doctors, for the perfecting of the saints, for the work of the ministry, for the edifying of the body of Christ" (Eph. IV.11–12). To these Christ promised the assistance of the Holy Ghost in order to make them safe guides in preaching, explaining, and defending the whole doctrine of Christ. Christ had transmitted orally to them the whole deposit of faith. He Himself did not write a line, not even for the use of His own Apostles. For more than three years He had been their teacher and He had promised and indeed sent them the Holy Ghost to teach them all truth, and to remind them of whatsoever He had taught them. We do not read anywhere that He ever ordered His Apostles to write; but He often reiterated His command to preach. Before the first book of the New Testament was written, that is, the Gospel of St. Matthew, Christians were counted by the thousands; churches had been founded in Palestine and elsewhere, and they flourished. These could not have been formed in any other way than by the oral teaching of the Apostles and their co-laborers in the vineyard of Christ; because the written word of the New Testament did not as yet exist. When written it was addressed to those, who were already instructed in the faith, as is clear from the titles of the Acts and of the letters of the Apostles. Matthew wrote his Gospel about 8 years after the Ascension of Christ, Mark 12 and Luke 20; John waited to write his Gospel until he was a very old man towards the end of the first century. Each one of them had a special purpose in view. Matthew wrote in Syro-Chaldaic for the special benefit of the Palestine Jews, to prove to them that Jesus was the promised Messiah, by showing that He was the Son of David and that all prophecies had been fulfilled in Him. Mark wrote his Gospel in Greek, while he was in Rome with Peter. He wrote at the request of the converted Romans to leave them a monument of Peter's preaching. Luke, a disciple and companion of Paul, wrote his Gospel in Achaia at the request of the Apostle. His purpose was to give the history of Christ more fully and ordinately for the special benefit of the converted Gentiles. He had learned what he wrote from the Apostles, and from the Blessed Virgin all that concerns the infancy and childhood of Jesus. John wrote his Gospel in the later years of his life, either on the island of Patmos or at Ephesus. He did so at the request of the bishops of Asia for the specific purpose of proclaiming the divine and human excellence of Jesus, to prove that He was indeed the Son of God and refute the errors that were creeping in.   In the Acts, Luke gives us the inspired history of the Primitive Church for a period of about 30 years after the Ascension of Christ.   The 14 epistles of St. Paul are addressed to individual churches or persons. The 7 universal or canonical epistles (1 of James, 2 of Peter, 3 of John, 1 of Jude) were addressed to the membership at large.   The Apocalypse of St. John is of all books of Scripture the hardest to understand. It is the last of the inspired writings.

Nowhere do we read of a commandment of Christ to His followers to read the Scriptures, but He did command them to listen to the preachers of the faith and to believe.   Faith comes from hearing, says St. Paul.   On one occasion Christ did say: Search the Scriptures (Jno. V.39). but He was then addressing the Jews, who had the Old Testament given to them for the purpose of preparing them for the coming of the Redeemer.   No writing could change the import of the apostolic preaching; St. Paul gives us the assurance of that: "Though we or an angel from heaven preach a gospel to you besides that which we have preached to you, let him be anathema" (Gal. 1.8).   Disobedience to the teaching authority, therefore, can never be explained away by an appeal to any other authority.

The religion of Jesus Christ, in whom alone salvation is to be found, and without whom there is no salvation, was established for all people of both sexes, of all ages and of every culture, of all times and of all places. Of the Christians of the first century many were illiterate, none of them could have had a copy of the whole inspired word; children and uncultured heathens could not have understood it rightly.

What importance did the Apostles themselves attach to writing? Did they all consign to writing their oral teaching? Was that a part of their Apostolate? If so, how did seven of them discharge their duties, since apparently they did not write a line? The Apostles had divided among themselves the then known world; each of them made numerous converts by his oral teaching alone. They never demanded of them the ability to read. Although in the beginning of the Church there were defects, as in all things human there ever will be, the followers of Christ were thorough Christians. They were converted Hebrews and Gentiles, who in the midst of the most terrible persecutions were always in danger of their lives; they were of one heart and one mind, and as such had the distinctive mark of disciples of Christ. The writings of the Apostles followed one another up to the end of the first century. Most of the Christians of the first century probably did not see any of these writings, but none saw them all; yet they were thorough Christians. The written word of the New Testament is only a compendium of the apostolic teaching; we cannot admit that it was all; they taught a great deal more than is recorded. The Apostles did not even record in writing all that Jesus did (Jno. XXI.25). Their teaching, whether written or unwritten, was infallible truth. If the apostolic writings were absolutely indispensable to the Christians of the first century, the faith of the Christians in later times must have been shocked when some of these writings disappeared. This seems to have happened. St. Paul in each of his two letters to the Corinthians alludes to letters, that have probably been lost. It is needless to say that the autographs of the Apostles did not last long after their death, on account of the troublesome times of the persecutions, and also because they were written on paper (2 Jno. 12), that is, on papyrus, the leaves of a quickly perishing plant. When probably the worse for use they were duplicated without the aid of a printing press, typewriter or carbon paper. These copyists were not guaranteed the assistance of the Holy Ghost, and most of the copies were probably defective in the one or other respect. Sometimes they added words. We have an illustration of that at the end of the Lord's prayer (Matt. VI.13) to which we find the following words attached: For thine is the kingdom, and the power, and the glory for ever. Christ did not utter these words, and yet they are attributed to Him in the English versions of the International Bible Agency.

The early Christians undoubtedly had the greatest respect for the Apostles, but it is not likely that the Christians of any particular church long possessed the privilege of having them in their midst. They must have looked with equal reverence almost upon those that had been directly put over them by the Apostles; these were holy men who held the affection of their flock. They may have written letters that were not inspired. How could the first Christians distinguish them from the truly inspired word? Discussions arose in the very early days, whether some of the writings of the one or other apostle were genuine or not. Neither Christ nor the Apostles had in their time the original text of the then existing inspired writings; they had the Greek text of the Septuagint or a translation of this. The only one that could have given them an authentic declaration of what constituted the written and inspired word of God in its entirety, was St. John, the last of the Apostles to leave the earth. St. John died without leaving them that catalogue.

The Apostles had unquestionably the highest regard for the written word. They knew it was the word of God Himself; they certainly imbued the first Christians with the deepest veneration for it. Did they consider it as a necessary and easy means for their followers to shape their faith? Although they lived in times nearer to the inspired authors, and amidst the traditions of their surroundings, was it easy for them to place the right interpretation upon it? Most of them would have answered with the Ethiopian: How can I understand unless some man show me? (Acts VIII.31.) St. Peter considered it his duty to warn his converts and all others concerning the epistles of his most dear brother Paul: "In all his epistles, speaking in them of these things; in which there are certain things hard to be understood, which the unlearned and unstable wrest, as they do also the other scriptures, to their own destruction" (2 Pet. III.16). We may conclude then that the early Christians could not have easy access to the written word and that the Apostles did not make the reading or study of it an essential condition for admission to membership in the Church.

Christ had commissioned His Apostles to teach all nations and to explain to them how to observe all things whatsoever He had commanded them (Matt. XXVIII.19-20). Christ had undoubtedly handed over the whole deposit of faith to the Church. We cannot for a moment doubt but that the Apostles were faithful dispensers of the ministry entrusted to them. They taught whatsoever Christ had commanded them for the propagation of His religion, and they did so by oral preaching. That same apostolic teaching was to be handed down to posterity in its entirety; part of it would not make up the whole teaching of Christ. Equal stress was therefore laid by the primitive Christians upon the means employed by the Apostles for the purpose. They did, as St. Paul ordered the Thessalonians to do: "Brethren: stand fast; and hold the traditions, which you have learned whether by word, or by our epistle" (2 Thes. II.14). This shows that the Apostles did not communicate their whole teaching in writing. The primitive Christians looked upon the written and oral word of the Apostles as of equal importance. As a matter of fact, the Christians of the first century had to be almost exclusively guided by Tradition, that is, by the word of God as passed on by speaking and hearing. If Tradition carried less weight than the written word, the first Christians would not have been as certain of their faith, as we are with both means at our disposal; this conclusion is unquestionably absurd.

Various means existed from the beginning for the safe transmission of the oral as well as for the written word. First of all they were directed by the public teaching of the living authority of the Church. This teaching had not only in its favor an undisputable human authority, but was also protected with immunity from error in all things appertaining to faith and morals. The articles of faith were presented to them in a concise form in the Symbols; such as the Symbol of the Apostles, which every adult Christian tried to memorize. Next came the liturgy or public worship and the public practice of the Church; the acts of the Martyrs; the writings of the early Fathers; the history of the heresies, always leading up to a clearer expression of the faith; a variety of other monuments, such as, paintings, sculptures, lapidary inscriptions, the tombs of the catacombs, and sacred buildings.

The authenticity and integrity of both the written and unwritten word were committed to the same authority, therefore both are equally safe means for the transmission of the Christian religion. This being so, there is no doubt but that divine Providence did safeguard the intact transmission of the one like of the other.

CHAPTER THIRTEENTH

DISPERSION OF THE APOSTLES AND FOUNDING OF THE CHURCH OF ANTIOCH

THE Acts do not tell us how many years after the Ascension of Christ the Apostles dispersed for the mission fields assigned to them. Various opinions, more or less founded, have been entertained in the past. Some writers at the end of the second century and at the beginning of the third spread a so-called tradition, according to which Christ had ordered His Apostles not to leave Jerusalem before the twelfth year after His death. This seems absurd, because we know from the Acts that Peter and John went before that time to Samaria to confirm the neophytes of Philip. The same source informs us also of Peter's pastoral tour to Joppe, Lydda, and other cities of Judea; after that he was called to Cesarea to instruct Cornelius. A constant tradition has always held that Peter first had his see at Antioch, and that he transferred it to Rome about the tenth year after Christ's Ascension. Baronius held that the Apostles dispersed after the martyrdom of James, which occurred about the tenth year after Christ's death, that Matthew wrote his Gospel before that time, that the cause of the dispersion was the murder of James, the imprisonment of Peter and the threat of Herod to put to death all the other Apostles. Some have gone so far as to think that the Apostles dispersed after the Council of Jerusalem, that is, after the year 47. The above opinions seem to be contradicted by more constant traditions, and by some texts of Scripture and by contemporary history. It has been constantly held that James the Greater was in Spain, undoubtedly before that date, because he had returned from his distant mission to Jerusalem and was martyred before then. That would place the dispersion about four years after Christ's death.

Christ had indeed commanded His Apostles to remain in Jerusalem until they had received the Holy Ghost. The order did not imply that they should leave immediately after that, yet, it is hard to imagine that all of them should have remained for ten long years among a perfidious and obstinate people, when they knew that the evangelization of the whole world had been entrusted to them. Moreover we know from the letter of St. Paul to the Galatians (I.19) that when he went to Jerusalem three years after his conversion, probably four years after Christ's death, he met, in the Holy City, Peter and James only; the others must have left before that.

It seems more probable that the Apostles dispersed shortly after the conversion of Cornelius; the barriers to the conversion of the heathens had then been removed by a clear manifestation of God's will. It is evident that as soon as God had manifested His will, they obeyed forthwith.

The Acts do not furnish a chronological survey of the chief events in the first half of the first century. We have before given the arguments of Cardinal De Lai in placing the death of Christ in year 29 of our era; this is the starting point of the Acts. Events followed one another in the following order:

That same year Peter converted 3000, and soon after 2000 more were added to the Church; the seven deacons were ordained; at the end of the year Stephen was stoned to death.

Two years later Saul was converted.

One or two years later, Peter converted Cornelius and opened the door of the Church to the Gentiles.

In 34, or 35 Peter established his see in Antioch; James went to Spain and the Apostles dispersed.

About the same time the famine predicted by Agabus at Antioch began to spread over the whole Roman empire.

Before 42, James returned from Spain to Jerusalem and was martyred by Herod Agrippa.

In 42, Peter was imprisoned and freed by an angel, and transferred his see from Antioch to Rome, where he died after an episcopate of 25 years.

In 47, the Council of Jerusalem was held.

We cannot vouch with absolute certainty for these figures, but they have in their favor the weightiest arguments.

The dispersion of the first Christians from Jerusalem, as a result of the persecution that arose on account of Stephen, the proto-martyr, led them as far as Phenice, Cyprus, and Antioch. Antioch was at that time the principal town of Syria, and ranked third in the whole Roman empire, following upon Rome and Alexandria. Antioch was then the seat of a Roman pro-consul; it flourished in arts and wealth, and counted many Jews among its citizens. The Church there was made up not only of converted Jews, but also of converts from paganism. St. Luke informs us that in this city the followers of Christ were first called Christians. As Jerusalem had been the center of the Judeo-Christians, so did Antioch become the center of the pagano-Christians. The early history of the Church at Antioch is of special importance from the fact that it was the See of the visible head of the Church, until he transferred it to Rome.

The first Christian refugees in Antioch spoke the Word, that is, preached the Gospel to the Jews only, but they were soon joined by other refugees from Cyprus and Cyrene, and these began to preach the Lord Jesus to the Greeks also. The Greeks here were not of those who had embraced Judaism; they were pagans. The Greeks at that time were masters of eloquence and philosophy; the word Greek then denoted not only nationality, but also great minds. St. Paul alluded to them as the wise, contrasted with the barbarians, who were the unwise (Rom. I.14). He tells us that the Greeks sought after wisdom (1 Cor. 1.22).

The Lord was with these new missionaries; their miracles, in confirmation of the faith which they preached with so much wisdom and zeal, converted many Gentiles. The good tidings soon came to the ears of the two Apostles then in Jerusalem, Peter and James. Neither of the two immediately proceeded to Antioch, for fear probably of offending the Jews in a familiar intercourse with the Gentiles from Cyprus and Antioch. In token of their approval of what had happened at Antioch, they sent Barnabas in their place. He was a native of Cyprus, and a Greek by birth, and therefore by communing with his own countrymen he could not give offence to the Jews. Barnabas was a good man, full of the Holy Ghost and of faith. On his arrival at Antioch he rejoiced at the wonders of grace, of which he saw so many living proofs before him; he was the man to encourage them to perseverance in their calling. He was destined to be the companion of Paul. From Antioch he went to Tarsus to seek Saul; both then returned to Antioch, and spent there a whole year. We have seen before that, although Peter was the first to receive the Gentiles into the church, Paul is rightfully called their Apostle; he was privileged to preach the Gospel over the whole Greco-Roman empire, and everywhere he gathered a rich harvest. The converted Jews did not look with particular favor upon him or upon his converts. Paul took up the defence of his heathen converts, when the others tried to place unjustifiable burdens upon them, or to treat them as inferiors. His fourteen epistles are a lasting monument of his love for them. The greater part of the primitive history of the Church, as recorded in the inspired Acts, is devoted to the work of the great Apostle of the Gentiles.

For the first four years after Christ, Jerusalem was the hub of religious activity, but it could not continue to be that. It was too far from the sea, difficult of access and eminently Jewish. This latter fact constituted rather a hindrance, when the Apostles realized that the stiff-necked Jews, as Stephen had called them, were not open to conviction, and that their chief efforts would henceforth be among the Gentiles. Luke gives us the details of the formation of a new center, more suitable to the supreme government of the Church than Jerusalem was. Antioch of Seleucia was admirably situated for that purpose. At the time of which we write it was a city of probably more than 500,000 inhabitants. It had gained immensely in importance since the Romans made it the capital of Syria. Political necessity and pleasing surroundings attracted people from all sides. But there was also another side to the picture; contemporary writers contend that in wickedness it competed with Corinth, the most infamous of all Greek cities.

The Jews, led by their inborn commercial instinct, were soon attracted by the profitable opportunities that presented themselves, under the encouragement of the Seleucians. Rivaling with the Ptolemies of Egypt, the Seleucians strove to gain the favor of the Jews. The Jews in Antioch therefore soon enjoyed the same privileges, as had been conferred upon them by the Alexandrians in Egypt. They could worship God in their synagogues, follow their own customs, and have their own chiefs not only in all religious, but also in many civil matters; they soon became very powerful. After the Romans had conquered Syria, they confirmed these privileges, and only sought to Romanize them and gain their hearts by a good administration.

The refugees from Jerusalem after the death of St. Stephen had followed the seashore; some had crossed over to Cyprus from some point in Phœnicia, the others had gone to Antioch. They were too sincere in their convictions and in their attachment to the religion of Jesus, not to act as missionaries in the cities and hamlets which they traversed; they had brought about many conversions in Antioch.

Paul was at Tarsus. What had he done after his conversion? He had gone into the desert of Arabia, a little south of Damascus, to ponder over God's great mercy in his regard, and prepare himself for the arduous task of the apostolate. On his return to Damascus he began to preach in the Jewish synagogues. The preaching of their former champion embittered the Jews; in their eyes he was an apostate. How could they oppose a man so learned, so convinced, and so zealous for the cause of Jesus? The only efficacious argument they could think of was to do away with him. They at once devised ways and means, with the connivance or positive help of King Aretas, to seize Paul and kill him. Paul had been an interested witness at the martyrdom of Stephen; a similar fate must have appealed to the love he bore his Master. The Christians in general were of a different opinion; they seemed to realize how valuable his services would be to the cause of Christianity; their wish prevailed. Paul was let down in a basket over the wall, and so escaped the dark designs of his former associates. They led Paul to Cæsarea, and thence by water to Tarsus. He was at that time unknown by face to the churches of Judea, but they had heard of him as a persecutor, and also of his subsequent conversion (Gal. I.21–24).

Paul was peacefully at work in Tarsus, when Barnabas who had made his acquaintance in Jerusalem, invited him to come to Antioch. The faithful there were called Christians, but they continued to call each other for quite a while yet—brother, chosen one, disciple, believer; not until the second century were they familiarly called Christians. Three times only does the name "Christian" appear in the New Testament. First in Antioch, when they were given the name; then when Herod Agrippa jokingly remarked to Paul: "In a little thou persuadest me to become a Christian" (Acts XXVI.28); and for the last time in the first epistle of St. Peter, where he exhorts the faithful to bear up with persecution willingly and to glorify God in the name of Christian (IV.16). In all probability that name was applied to the followers of Christ, not by the Jews, but by the heathens. It must have been a byword of the Antiochians, when they saw that the little party, consisting of a few Jews and a few Gentiles, in their eyes both uncultured and fanatic, proceeded to the conquest of the world, when so many stronger parties had failed.

Barnabas and Paul had made many converts, and

a great multitude was added to the Lord (Acts XI.24). The gains did not form a new Church, but were simply added to the existing Church, like on the day of Pentecost.

The inspired narrative does not connect the name of Peter with the founding of the church at Antioch. Yet we know from the most accredited sources that Peter was Bishop of Antioch. We find that constant tradition corroborated by the testimony of three great writers, all prior to the second half of the fifth century. Eusebius the great historian tells us that after founding the Church of Antioch, Peter went to Rome, where he continued as bishop for 25 years. St. John Chrysostom born in Antioch has always been considered as the great light of the Eastern church. In addressing his fellow-citizens he told them: "This is one of the honorable prerogatives of our city that it had from the very beginning the Prince of the Apostles as teacher. It was indeed proper that that city, receiving before all others the name of Christian, should have had for pastor the chief of the Apostles. But we did not keep him for ever, we gave him over to the royal city of Rome."

St. Jerome, who died in 420, says: Peter, the Prince of the Apostles, after his episcopate in the church of Antioch, went to Rome in the second year of Claudius, and continued there for 25 years up to the end of his life in the fourteenth year of Nero.

It was evidently not the purpose of the sacred writer to record all occurrences, however important they might seem. There is nothing in the narrative, which precludes the founding of that Church by St. Peter. We have seen him visiting the dispersed Christians, and nothing prevents us from believing that he went up to visit the refugees from Jerusalem and Cyprus, organized the Church and left Mark in charge, when he left. Tradition has it that Peter held the see of Antioch for seven years, until he removed it to Rome, but this does not compel us to believe that he resided in these places uninterruptedly; we know the contrary to be true; his office of supreme shepherd frequently demanded his presence elsewhere.

The Church had not only Apostles, but also Prophets; prophecy was one of the gifts of the Holy Ghost. Prophets were sent from Jerusalem to Antioch to confirm the flourishing church in the faith by their gift of prophecy. One of them, Agabus by name, foretold a great famine over the whole world, which came to pass under Claudius. The Holy Ghost willed that Christian prophets should foretell this famine, lest the heathens should ascribe the cause to Christianity and call for the wrath of their pagan gods. Christ had foretold persecutions to his followers, lest they weakheartedly should take them as occasions to shake their faith. Another reason why the Holy Ghost had the famine foretold was that the Christians of Antioch might send relief to their unfortunate brethren in Judea, as actually they did through the hands of Barnabas and Saul. The whole Roman Empire deserved to be punished for its crimes, especially for the idolatry of Caius Caligula, the emperor who preceded Claudius; he insisted upon being adored as god, and not be second even to Jupiter, whose image he wished to change into his own. He had his statue erected in the temple of Jerusalem, and demanded adoration even from the Jews. The Jews indeed remonstrated, but they also deserved to be punished for their persecution of Christ and of His Apostles. The famine came in the second year of the reign of Claudius; the gifts of the Antiochians were sent to the ancients —the presbyters, which shows that Jerusalem had its priests.

CHAPTER FOURTEENTH

DEATH OF ST. JAMES AND IMPRISONMENT
OF ST. PETER

DURING the famine under Emperor Claudius, King Herod started a fresh persecution against the Church in Jerusalem. This Herod had been educated in Rome, where he had made the acquaintance of Claudius. There are four Herods mentioned in the New Testament: Herod the Ascalonite, the murderer of the infants at Bethlehem; Herod Antipas, who beheaded St. John and mocked Christ during His passion; Herod Agrippa, who murdered St. James and imprisoned St. Peter; Herod Agrippa Jr., who ruled at the time of the destruction of Jerusalem, and to whom Josephus dedicated his history of the Jewish people.

The new persecution was not fomented as before by the Sanhedrim or by the Jewish people, but by the king himself, to whom power over life and death had been given by the Romans. His motive was not hatred of Christianity or zeal for the law of Moses; it was a political move. Soon after the martyrdom of St. James, God showed by the deliverance of Peter and the punishment of Herod, that everything is subject to his power, and that He is the protector and the avenger of His Church.

Why was James selected as the victim of Herod's cruelty? The James of whom we now treat is James the Greater, the brother of John and one of the three specially favored Apostles. He was one of the chief pillars of the Church. Most probably he was the Apostle of Spain, where he is supposed to have converted two famous magicians to the faith. It is quite likely that the numerous Jews in Spain at that time took great offence at his success and induced their brethren in Jerusalem to do away with him; James was a convincing opponent of Judaism. He was murdered shortly before Easter. Herod beheaded James, as his grand-uncle had beheaded John the Baptist. There are but few instances in the Old Testament of the Jews using the sword, but since they had fallen under the yoke of the Romans, they had adopted this manner of execution. Ancient history supplements some interesting details to the inspired narrative. St. Clement according to Eusebius wrote that his executioner, when leading him to the place of execution, was so moved by his bravery in the midst of all the indignities heaped upon him, that he proclaimed himself a Christian. On the way he asked James' pardon. After a moment's deliberation James told him: Peace be to you, and he embraced him; both were beheaded. St. Isidore adds that on his way to martyrdom, James restored perfect health to a paralytic. He was the first of the Apostles to die; his brother John survived all the other Apostles and died in the beginning of the second century.

James, as son of Zebedee and Mary Salome, was related to Christ.

Herod had gained his purpose in the murder of James; it pleased the Jews, who in the beginning of his reign were rather prejudiced against him on account of the pagan customs he acquired in Rome. The Jews in Jerusalem must have known by that time that Peter was the head of what they considered a new sect; his capture and extinction would be looked upon with still greater favor. King and people most probably thought that by putting the leader out of the way, they could easily seize the other Apostles, and completely uproot the new religion. Herod arranged therefore to seize Peter; on account of the feast of Easter he imprisoned him, and gave him in charge of four files of soldiers, with the intention to bring him forth to the people at the end of the seven days of the unleavened bread. James was killed before the pasch, in order not to sully by his blood the festive days. The purpose of bringing Peter before the people after Easter meant a sentence of death.

The Church was not insensible to the treatment meted out to its supreme shepherd. The prayers of all the faithful went up to heaven on his behalf. The united prayer was efficacious; a miracle delivered Peter out of the hands of Herod. With the Romans four soldiers constituted a guard. During the night they were on duty for three hours, when they were relieved by four others; four files were therefore required for the night watch. God waited to interfere up to the last moment, when Herod was about to bring him forth. God was with Peter in his tribulations, but delayed relief until humanly speaking, the case seemed hopeless, to teach Peter and all His children to trust in Him, however desperate conditions may appear: His will shall prevail, even though a miracle is required.

All possible precautions had been taken to prevent Peter's escape. Two soldiers were with him on the inside of the prison and two on guard on the outside; he was bound with two chains, each of the two soldiers holding one; all human possibility of escape had vanished. Peter felt so comfortable in his confidence in God that he had fallen asleep. All of a sudden an angel in human form stood by him; his assumed body lighted up the room. The angel struck Peter on the side and raised him up and said to him: "Arise quickly, gird thyself, and put on thy sandals." The chains immediately fell from his hands. The angel added: "Cast thy garment about thee and follow me." Peter obeyed; he was not aware that he had an angel as leader; he thought it was a vision. They passed through the first and second ward, guarded by soldiers, who did not notice the passers-by. The iron gate of the city opened of itself to them; they passed on through one more street, and immediately the angel departed from Peter.

Peter then came to himself and realized what had happened, how the Lord by an angel had delivered him out of the hands of Herod, and from all the expectation of the Jewish people. At dawn as soon as the flight was discovered, there was no small stir among the soldiers; they wondered what had happened to Peter; Herod looked for him in vain. Taking revenge upon the guards, he commanded that they be put to death for having let his prey escape. He thought further to appease his wrath on the Tyrians and on the Sidonians, who pleaded for mercy. On the day appointed for Herod to hear their case he appeared arrayed in royal apparel and made a speech to the assembly. In the spirit of flattery his hearers told him that his voice was that of a god, not of a man. His measure of iniquity was full; the angel struck him forthwith, because he had claimed for himself the honor that belonged to God. His grandfather, Herod the Ascalonite, the murderer of the innocent babes at Bethlehem, had been consumed by fleas before death; the grand-son was being eaten by worms before he died.

Meanwhile after Peter had come to and the angel had departed from him, he came to the house of Mary, the mother of John surnamed Mark, who was a companion to Barnabas and Paul on their mission tours. Many of the faithful were gathered in Mary's house and fervently prayed for Peter. Peter knocked on the outside gate; a little girl named Rhode came to hear who the stranger was. She recognized Peter's voice, but she was so overcome with joy that she forgot to open the gate, but ran back with the message to the assembled faithful. They did not believe her. Peter kept on knocking. They finally opened the gate and to their great astonishment they saw Peter really and truly. Peter entered and beckoned to them to hold their peace and listen. He explained how the Lord had delivered him, and requested them to carry the news to James and the brethren in Jerusalem. The message to James shows that he was then the only Apostle in Jerusalem.

The inspired writer of the Acts concludes his narrative of Peter's deliverance from prison with the following sentence: "And going out he went into another place" (XII.17). Which is that other place? St. Luke does not tell us, but nearly all sacred writers of the first few centuries after Christ surmise that the goal of his journey was the city of Rome. St. Luke probably does not mention the fact because it was well known to Theophilus, a citizen of Rome as many claim, whom he was addressing in his Acts. Ancient writers inform us that Peter passed through Cæsarea, Sidon, Antioch, Galatia, Cappadocia, and many other places, where he confirmed the faithful and appointed bishops, until he came to Rome, where he founded a church in the house of a senator.

CHAPTER FIFTEENTH

THE importance of Jerusalem as a center of Christian activity was soon superseded by Antioch, situated far more conveniently, and animated by a much better spirit, in a community which was called before all others Christian. Peter in the meantime had established his see elsewhere. A new and prominent figure now appeared on the scene. That figure is Paul of Tarsus, to whose apostolic labors, Luke devotes the rest of his inspired chapters, with the exception of one important event—the Council of Jerusalem. Barnabas had invited Paul to Antioch, which harbored then prophets and doctors of the New Dispensation. Among them were Barnabas, Simon, surnamed Niger, Lucius of Cyrene, and Manahen who was a foster brother of Herod the Tetrarch, and Saul (Acts XXIII.1).

Barnabas and Saul were selected at the inspiration of the Holy Ghost for more important work. The inspired writer adds: Then they fasting and praying and imposing their hands upon them, sent them away. (XIII.3) It would seem that by the imposition of hands episcopal consecration is meant. With one exception; viz., when Christ is asked to impose His

hands on little children (Matt. XIX.13) that rite in
the New Testament is always used, either to cure or to
consecrate, as in the ordination of deacons, in the administration of Confirmation, in episcopal consecration, etc.   Most commentators of Holy Scripture contend that Barnabas and Saul were consecrated bishops
by the imposition of hands.   The fact that prayer and
fasting accompanied and preceded that rite seems to
confirm that view.   In their Apostolate Barnabas and
Saul certainly acted as bishops, and we do not read
anywhere else of their consecration.   Paul indeed
wrote to the Galatians (II.6) that the Apostles added
nothing to him, but this must be understood of the
doctrine and the gospel, which he learned directly
from Christ, not from the Apostles.   Ananias baptized him, the Apostles confirmed him and ordained
him a priest.   Christ directly consecrated His Apostles bishops; they and their successors were to consecrate all others.   Who was the Apostle or Bishop
that consecrated Barnabas and Saul?   Not Peter
who was on his way to Rome, nor James the Greater
who had been martyred by Herod, nor some of the
Apostles who were out on distant missions, but
James the bishop of Jerusalem may have been invited
or John or Matthias; perhaps some of the prophets or
doctors in the Church of Antioch may have been
bishops.

Paul longed to preach the Gospel in his native Asia
Minor, Barnabas held out for his native island of
Cyprus, and won in the holy contest.   Being sent by
the Holy Ghost they first went to Seleucia, the sea-

port of Antioch, and a very important commercial town, whence they could conveniently sail over to Cyprus. They landed in Salamina on the east coast of the island. They began to preach in the synagogues of the Jews, in order not to offend them unnecessarily. They had with them John Mark, the son of Mary, at whose house Peter knocked after his deliverance out of the hands of Herod. John Mark was a cousin german of Barnabas, who had and showed a special affection for him; this affection was so intense that it caused him to prefer his company to that of Saul. Whether this Mark of whom we read in the Acts and in the letters of St. Paul is the same as the Mark of the second gospel, and whom St. Peter calls his son, that is, his spiritual disciple (I Pet. V.13) is another question, but of little importance. In order to relieve himself of many cares, Saul could have left the economic question in the hands of pious women, who helped the other Apostles and Peter (1 Cor. IX.15). But he wished to be free and not to be a burden to any one; he did not care to have any one throw up to him support by others, when he himself had been so outspoken, as to say: "If any man will not work, neither let him eat" (Thes. III.10). He was far from blaming the other Apostles for the practice, which they had adopted; for himself he wished to be independent of all, in order to be able to tell the truth more forcibly to all. We will find him on his journeys preaching the Gospel in daytime, and making mats at night. He traveled from place to place, generally on foot, and lived on the plainest fare. In doing so he exposed himself to all sorts of hardships and dangers. Clement of Rome attests that Paul fell several times into the hands of highway robbers. The sea even had dangers of its own. Paul sums up all his trials in his second letter to the Corinthians (XI.23–24). In addition to the above he had the solicitude of all the churches. The worst torture for him was the sting of the flesh to buffet him; he was subject to the concupiscence of the flesh, perhaps more violently than ordinary mortals are. However pleasing he was to God, and favored by Him, God would not relieve him of tribulation; it was to be the battle of a lifetime, but coöperation with grace would bring victory.

In a little over 20 years the zealous Apostle will go from city to city, all the way from Syria to Spain. Paul and the other Apostles experienced that numerous and powerful groups of Jews, located in various parts were of great advantage to them. These had as a rule their own quarters, presided over by a religious chief; the ghettoes of the Middle Ages and of later times were but another term for them. Jewish travelers carried letters of recommendation from place to place; the ghetto contributed to the diffusion of the Gospel. It is then quite natural that Paul's first sermon in a place should be delivered in a synagogue. At these meetings the stranger and the guest always had the preference.

The Acts do not disclose what the results of the preaching at Salamina were; we are led to believe that the stay of the missionaries at Salamina was short

and the results insignificant. They crossed the whole
island; better spiritual consolations awaited them at
Paphos on the west coast. This place was the home
of the pro-consul Sergius Paul. He was an intelligent
man, but he had fallen under the influence of a Jew
named Barjesu, who called himself an Elymas—a
magician (XIII.8). Occult sciences had their attraction then as they have now; some used them with
more or less charlatanism in connection with the
hidden forces of nature; others tried to unveil a world
entirely unknown. These occult sciences were very
much in favor in the Orient at that time; the Orient
had been the cradle of the great religions, and also
of great superstitions. The best minds were not
always immune against the common contagion. So
had Sergius Paul fallen under the fascinating influence of Barjesu. God drew good from evil; the
pro-consul's curiosity for the unknown led him
into the arms of Saul and Barnabas, as soon as he
learned that they were messengers of a new doctrine. The magician tried to paralyze the impression made on Sergius; he realized what loss Sergius' conversion to Christianity would mean to
himself; religion for him was but a cloak. Saul filled
with the Holy Ghost looking upon him said: "O
full of all guile and of all deceit, child of the devil,
enemy of all justice, thou ceasest not to pervert the
right ways (XIII.10). In the name of God, and as a
punishment he was struck with temporary blindness.
Sergius Paul had allowed himself to be misled by the
magician, but in the presence of a real wonderworker

the scales fell from his eyes and he believed. In connection with this wonderful conversion the Acts remind us that Saul was also called Paul, and after that the name of Paul is always given to the Apostle of the Gentiles. Some of the early commentators, and among them St. Jerome, were of the opinion that Saul on this occasion changed his name into Paul, in memory of his first illustrious convert. It is, however, more likely that his parents at Tarsus, then part of Rome's dominions, had given him a name, which in Hebrew was Saul and with the Romans Paul, to use according to his relations with either society.

Paul had first yielded to Barnabas in the evangelization of his native island, but the rôles will be from now on inverted; Paul looked for a broader field. Henceforth he will not entertain any relation with Cyprus; Barnabas alone will return to the island and earnestly endeavor to convert it. In the future, not Paul will follow Barnabas, but Barnabas Paul as a disciple follows his master.

The missionary band left the island and set sail for the western shore of Asia Minor to Pamphilia, and going up a river they passed through Perge, a city that entertained commercial relations with Paphos, and proceeded to Antioch of Pisidia. The town should not be confused with the more famous Antioch of Seleucia, where the followers of Christ were first called Christians.

Asia Minor was then divided into several small regions, not all equally civilized and some of which still enjoyed a limited independence, but the Roman eagles extended their wings over all. The Jews were very numerous in these parts, and in that regard Asia Minor ranked third, after Egypt and Cyrenaica.

The Apostles did not tarry long in Perge, which at that season of the year was very unhealthy. That is perhaps the reason why John Mark departed from them and returned to Jerusalem. If this John Mark is not the later disciple of St. Peter and the Evangelist, we may suppose that he found the Apostolate demanded more sacrifices than he had anticipated, when he accompanied his cousin Barnabas to Cyprus. Perhaps he was too much attached to Jewish traditions to relish the idea of Paul's work among the Gentiles. His departure grieved Barnabas. Paul considered him too light spiritually.

Paul and Barnabas proceeded to Antioch of Pisidia. On the first sabbath day they entered the synagogue and sat down. After the reading of the law and of the prophets, the rulers of the synagogue sent word to the Apostles to address the congregation, if they had any word of exhortation to offer. Paul eagerly seized the opportunity, and bespeaking silence with his hand, he delivered a long discourse, which we find recorded in Chapter XIII of the Acts. This is the first recorded speech of St. Paul. As it would be childish to assert that every word of Paul is recorded, so it would be equally unchristian and erroneous to imagine that Paul did not develop the points indicated by the author of the Acts. To captivate the benevolence of his hearers Paul began by mentioning some of God's many favors to their race. He had chosen their forefathers to be the leaders of his chosen people; He was with them, when they were sojourners in Egypt, and brought them out of that land of bondage; He bore up with their perversity and fed them in the desert; He made them conquer their enemies, gave them judges and prophets, and kings at their request. Paul mentions one in particular, David, the man according to God's own heart. He then treats of the Precursor, John the Baptist. After that introduction, he proved that Jesus is indeed the Messiah, and insisted that in Christ alone remission of sins and justification can be obtained, and not in the Old Law; also that faith is an essential condition to salvation. The immediate result of Paul's speech was that at the end of the meeting the Apostles were requested to address them again on the following sabbath. In the meantime Paul and Barnabas requested them to be steadfast in their newly acquired convictions. During the week the Apostles had occasion to preach Christ to the many Gentiles in Antioch. The next Sabbath almost the whole town went to hear the Apostles; there were many Gentiles in the audience. Their presence filled the Jews with envy; they began blasphemously to contradict the Apostles. These in reply gave them to understand that it was proper for them to preach first to the Jews, but as they rejected the word of God, they would turn to the Gentiles. The Jews had judged themselves unworthy of eternal life, their places were taken by the Gentiles. The Acts do not state that all the pagans, who had listened to Paul, were converted and believed, but only those that were ordained to life everlasting. God's call to the faith is also a call to life eternal, which cannot be obtained without faith. Man's free will remains unimpaired through God's merciful call; as all hearers of Christ's word did not submit to His teaching, so not all are converted by the plea of the Apostles.

The Jews, in this instance, resorted to an hitherto unknown form of opposition; they stirred up religious and honorable women, as also the chief men of the city against the Apostles. St. Jerome some 300 years later tells us that up to his time, women had played a conspicuous part as abettors of heresy. To mention only one instance, it is well known that Simon the Magician had a notorious woman as auxiliary. These women at Antioch were successful in raising a storm against Paul and Barnabas; the Jews finally cast them out of their coasts. The Apostles carried out the injunction of their Master, and shook off the dust of their feet against them. This symbolic act meant that in future they would have nothing more in common with them; they would leave it to God's vengeance to deal with them. The ejected Apostles did not lose courage, nor did their neophytes. They were filled with joy in the midst of their tribulations and with new graces of the Holy Ghost to strengthen them in the fight with the opponents of their religious convictions.

Paul and Barnabas went to Iconium, south-east of Antioch. They began their missionary work exactly as they had done in other places. Paul preached to

Jews and Gentiles in the Synagogue; the Gentiles were admitted in Antioch. In the temple of Jerusalem, as planned by Herod, there was just outside of the wall enclosing the sanctuary, a court of the Gentiles. The sacred writer informs us that a very great multitude of both Jews and Gentiles were converted. One of the most illustrious converts was Thecla, a fair young lady of a wealthy family. She had been betrothed by her mother to a rich and noble young man. He was a heathen like herself before she embraced Christianity. She had learned from the Apostle to value virginity above matrimony, and therefore refused to abide by her mother's decision. Her mother and the young man brought her before heathen judges; Thecla endured the most horrible tortures, but she remained unmoved. All the early Fathers sing her praises. Paul here also converted Tryphaena and Tryphosa, to whom he sent greetings in his letter to the Romans (XVI.12) and whom he praised for their great work in the Church in Rome, like formerly in Iconium.

Soon in Iconium persecution broke out in a new form. Up to now all hostile acts against the Church had been planned and executed exclusively by the Jews. This time the unbelieving Jews excited the Gentiles against the Apostles. Their argument was that the Apostles endeavored to add to the Roman collection of gods a new one, and a crucified Jew at that.

The Apostles remained for a long time at Iconium; probably for two reasons, first, because the very great multitude of converts demanded their ministry; second, because the Jews had incensed the Gentiles against them; they remained longer in order to convert them by their constancy, zeal, and miracles. In the Acts Paul and Barnabas are here for the first time called Apostles. Barnabas was not an Apostle in the strict sense, like Paul and the Twelve, because he was not directly called by Christ; he had perhaps not seen the risen Christ and therefore was not an eye witness of the Resurrection. These two conditions were required for the Apostolate strictly speaking; he was therefore an Apostle in the broader sense.

The people at Iconium were divided in their feelings towards the Apostles. Their opponents decided to use them contumeliously, and to stone them. The Apostles who were informed of their intention fled south to Lystra and Derbe, and they evangelized the whole country around. A miracle at Lystra gained the admiration of the people for them. Paul had among his hearers a cripple from birth; he looked upon him and seeing that he had the faith, which Our Lord usually demanded as a preliminary for a cure, told him with a loud voice: "Stand upright on thy feet." The man leaped up and walked; a miracle had been wrought. The people were so excited that they proclaimed aloud in their patois, which Paul probably did not understand, that the gods had come down in the likeness of men. A proof that Paul had not understood them is that he did not immediately rebuke them. This is not inconsistent with the gift of languages which he had received. The use of that gift presupposes in the minds of speakers and hearers an actual motion of the Holy Ghost; this motion was transitory, not ever present.

The people called Barnabas Jupiter, and Paul Mercury. Barnabas ranked higher in their estimation, because he was physically superior to Paul. In pagan mythology Mercury is Jupiter's son; he was considered the god of eloquence, the companion and interpreter of Jupiter. Jupiter had his temple near the city; there was a priest attached to it. This priest brought out oxen, and garlands to adorn the victims, the priest, and the ministers. The victims were to be offered at the gate of the city, to enable all the people to be present at the sacrifice. When Paul and Barnabas had learned their purpose, they rent their garments in Jewish fashion to express their abhorrence for this blasphemy and sacrilege, and leaping among the people they addressed them sternly. They told them that they were but mortals like all of.them, and that it was their special mission to convert them from these vain things—from their sacrifices to Jupiter and Mercury to the living God, to whom alone sacrifice can be offered. The people were so enthused that the Apostles could hardly restrain them from offering sacrifice to them. It was a repetition of Palm Sunday and Good Friday, and showed again human fickle-mindedness and unreliableness.

The jealous Jews of Antioch and Iconium had heard in the meantime of the Apostles' wonderful success at Lystra. They sent their men there to tell the people that Paul and Barnabas were not the messengers of new gods, but of demons, and that they would bring the direst calamities upon the city, and that therefore they deserved to be stoned. The people's minds were poisoned, and Paul was stoned. Paul was singled out, because he had been the spokesman; he suffered in his body the same tortures which he had inflicted before on Stephen; but he was Saul then, he is Paul now. They dragged what they thought a corpse, out of the city to avoid contamination. The disciples stood round about the body, to bury Paul, if he were dead, or to hide him from the fury of the Jews, if he lived. Paul rose, he had been cured instantaneously, and he returned to the city. The Acts do not furnish any details of what happened in the city on Paul's return. The sacred writer left it to the imagination of his readers to reproduce the scene—the joy of the neophytes and the confusion of the others.

The next day Paul and Barnabas left for Derbe. They preached the Gospel to that city, and taught many; no other particular occurrences are mentioned. The Apostles then retraced their steps towards Antioch, everywhere exhorting their followers to continue in the faith. These exhortations show that the Apostles did not believe that those who had received the faith could not lose it; they made no secret of it that but one road leads to the kingdom of God, and that is the royal road of the cross. Persecution is to be expected by all those, who wish to live piously in Christ Jesus, as St. Paul clearly states in his second letter to Timothy (III.12). To continue their work the Apostles after praying and fasting ordained priests for the various churches and bishops for the larger cities. As we have explained above (Chapter XI) the word presbyter—elder—applies in the New Testament to priests of the first and second order.

The Apostles had not visited Attalia on the way up, they do so on their return to take the boat for Antioch. This concluded the first journey of St. Paul. At Antioch they related to the assembled faithful the episodes of their journey, and how God had opened the door of faith to the Gentiles through the grace of the Holy Ghost and the preaching of the Apostles. The Acts tell us that they remained no small time with the disciples at Antioch, probably up to their departure for the Council of Jerusalem.

CHAPTER SIXTEENTH

ST. PETER IN ROME

THE truth of a historical fact rests upon the evidence of unimpeachable witnesses. Its truth and certainty are not impaired by some connecting details that are hard to explain. The coming of St. Peter to Rome is one of these historical facts. It has in its favor the most convincing proofs, that should satisfy the most exacting critic. To deny or to doubt it would mean a total ignorance of the literature of the Church in the first century. It is true that the inspired word of God—the Acts and the letters of the Apostles—do not express it in so many words.

The historical purpose of the Acts is to relate the founding of the Church among the Jews, the Samaritans, and the Gentiles, but the chief purpose was to illustrate the divine origin of the Christian religion and of the Church. It would be absurd to look in the Acts for a chronological and complete enumeration of the chief events in the early Church, or of the deeds of each Apostle. The writer of the Acts was a companion of Paul, at whose request he also wrote a Gospel; it is quite natural that Luke should rather give a history of Paul, and defend his authority.

As the Acts were addressed to the faithful in Rome, it was unnecessary to mention an historical fact known to all.

The same applies to the epistles of Paul, and especially to the one he addressed to the Romans. This letter was probably written in Achaia in the year 53, after Claudius, in the ninth year of his reign, had expelled the Jews from Rome, and Peter with them. There was no need of mentioning Peter, when Paul knew that he was not there. We gather from Paul's other epistles that he did not send them to the bishops, and that he did not even send them greetings. Paul had his own messengers. He sent his letter to the Romans by Phoebe, a deaconess of a church near Corinth, and a very prominent woman in her own land, who had to undertake a business journey to Rome. What more natural but that such a messenger would first call on Peter, if he had been there, and given him all the news about his dear brother Paul.

In the last chapter of the Acts we are told that the Jews in Rome wished to have Paul's views about the sect that was being contradicted everywhere (XXVIII.22). It might appear that if Peter had been there the Jews would not have been so absolutely ignorant of the Christian religion. We know from Paul himself that before he came to Rome, there was a most flourishing community there, the faith of which was known all over the world. It is not likely that the unconverted Jews were admitted to the meetings of the Christians in private houses. It is therefore quite possible that they were totally ignorant of what they call the sect, and desired information from Paul. These and a few more similar passages do not prove indeed that Peter was in Rome, but at the same time they do not disprove it.

Is it true that the New Testament is entirely reticent about a fact of that importance, concerning the chief of the Apostles? We think not. The New Testament gives us the first proof of that fact in the first epistle of Peter, wherein he says: "The Church that is in Babylon, elected together with you, saluteth you, and so does my son Mark" (V.13). Peter was then in Babylon. Where was this Babylon? Was it Babylon in Egypt, Babylon in Chaldea, or the provice of Babylon? The ancient interpreters unanimously took Babylon for pagan Rome, which was then the harlot standing on the seven hills. That Babylon had been drenched with the blood of the martyrs of Jesus (Ap. XVII); this applies to neither of the other two Babylons. Pagan Rome was called Babylon in the mystic language of the first Christians, on account of her idolatry and general corruption. No one has ever attempted to prove that Peter went as far east as the Euphrates; his presence was not particularly required there, because there were but few Christians among the Parthians. Many modern critics, otherwise hostile to Christianity, like Renan, concede that the letter of St. Peter was written in Rome.

We find another allusion to the same fact in the letter of St. Paul to the Romans. He says that he refrained from going to Rome up to then "lest he should build upon another man's foundation" (Rom. XV.20–22). There must have been another founder of the Roman Church, and one so conspicuous that Paul out of respect for him abstained from visiting the capital of the Roman Empire. He must have been an Apostle; Christian tradition never attributed the foundation of the Roman Church to any other but Peter.

The place of Peter's death and also the kind of his martydom must have been well known to the Christians of the first century. Christ had foretold by what death Peter should glorify God (Jno. XXI.19). A fact so notorious in the days of the Apostles maintained its notoriety in the following generation and could not have been altered or transformed a little while afterwards. If Peter died in Babylon, all contemporary Christians would have known it, and it was morally impossible that shortly afterwards the opinion should have prevailed that Peter came to Rome and died there.

We do not here inquire how long Peter resided in Rome, but simply establish the fact that he was there. According to constant tradition he was Bishop of Rome for 25 years. This, however, does not mean that he resided there uninterruptedly. We know that when the Jews were expelled, he also was obliged to leave, and did not return until that decree of expulsion was rescinded. We must also admit that his office of chief shepherd frequently demanded his presence elsewhere, while he remained Bishop of Rome.

The weight of evidence is such that few facts of history are better corroborated. For the present we will give only the proofs of his coming to Rome and of his residence there. None of the ancients ever contended that Peter went to Rome before he had been cast into prison by Herod Agrippa about the feast of Easter in 42. Josephus tells us that when Claudius came to the throne in January 41, he appointed Herod king of the whole of Palestine. In the following year Peter was delivered out of his dungeon, left Palestine and went into another place (Acts XII.17). This other place was Rome. Herod died in 43. Peter must have gone to Rome the previous year, because, according to the very oldest documents, like the Chronicon of Eusebius and the writings of St. Jerome, Mark who acted as Peter's secretary or interpreter, left Rome for Alexandria in the third year of Claudius, after he had written his Gospel in Rome.

Horace Marucchi, one of the greatest archeologists of our times, sees in a letter of St. Clement to the Corinthians the most ancient document proving the martyrdom of St. Peter in Rome. Clement was bishop of Rome from 90 to 100; Hegesippus, Irenæus, and Eusebius all speak of that letter, the text of which had been lost for a long time. It was recovered in London and printed in 1633. In that precious document, written in 96 or 97, mention is made of the two Apostles—Peter and Paul. Clement wrote from Rome and in the name of the Church of Rome. The mention of the two names along with other illustrious persons "amongst us," as Clement expressed it, is of the highest importance, and is an allusion to the then well known fact of Peter's coming into the capital of the Cæsars.

A few years later under the reign of Trajan, Ignatius, bishop of Antioch and condemned to die in the Roman ampitheater, wrote his famous letter to the Romans. In it he begs of them not to intercede to save his life and he adds: I do not command it like Peter and Paul; they were Apostles, I am but a slave. Here again there is no explicit proof of the coming of St. Peter to Rome, but his mention together with St. Paul is an evident allusion to that fact, not a mere insinuation of it. Insinuation may be made of a fact not well known; to a fact universally known allusion is made.

After these indirect proofs come the more numerous and positive proofs, from the second century onward.

Irenæus was a disciple of Polycarp, who himself had been a disciple of St. John. He knew the churches of Asia, and as bishop in Gaul he often had occasion to visit Rome on important business. Polycarp had known the Apostles and especially St. John; he had lived with John and others who had seen Christ. He must have learned from St. John, not only the manner of Peter's martyrdom, but also the place. He recorded the manner in his Gospel several years after Peter's death. John survived

Peter for more than 30 years. Who will deny that John knew and communicated to Polycarp the place? Could Irenæus have had a more unmistakable source of information for what he wrote? In his book "Against Heresies" Irenæus says: As it would be too long to enumerate in this my book, the succession of pastors in all the churches, we will indicate that succession for the Church of Rome, founded and organized by the too glorious Apostles— Peter and Paul. By the succession of its bishops we confound all who differ from us. In that church the faithful of all places can learn the apostolic tradition. After having founded and instructed that church, the two Apostles gave over the administration of it to Linus. Anaclet succeeded Linus; Clement was the third from the Apostles to obtain that episcopate. . . . Now (at the time of Irenæus' writing) the twelfth from the Apostles to be Bishop of Rome was Eleutherius. He as successor of Peter ruled the Church of Rome for 15 years and died in 193.

St. Denis of Corinth, who preceded Irenæus by a few years, was a great man in his day and died in 170. He wrote to the Romans: "Both Apostles instructed us in Corinth, together they left for Italy, and after preaching the faith endured martyrdom at the same time."

Origen for Alexandria and Tertullian for Africa attest explicitly that Peter founded the Church of Rome. Finally Eusebius, the historian of the time of Constantine, affirms the same in various parts of his history.

Besides the many historical proofs, direct and indirect, there is another argument of the highest importance. It is the fact that none of the early Christian Churches ever protested the claims of the Roman Church; that Church has always claimed to have been founded by Peter and to possess his grave. If Peter did not die in Rome he must have died somewhere else. Wherever that happened, his grave would have been looked upon as a sanctuary, and the city that possessed his remains would have gloried in the fact. But from the very beginning Rome alone claimed Peter's tomb; no other city ever disputed that claim. Both the Eastern and the Western Church have accepted the fact.

CHAPTER SEVENTEENTH

THE COUNCIL OF JERUSALEM

THE Gospel had been preached throughout the greater part of Asia Minor; the evangelical seed had sprouted everywhere, but it had produced an especially rich harvest in the capital of Syria—Antioch. The inspired writer does not tell us how many adherents the Church counted about 17 years after the Ascension of Christ. If we add to the results obtained by Peter, Paul, Barnabas, the deacon Philip, whose work is mentioned in the Acts, the harvest of souls brought into the fold by the other eleven Apostles in various parts of the world, of which no mention is made, we can readily imagine that there must have been many thousands, all converts from Judaism or paganism. As long as the converts represented only one race—the Jews—they were all of one heart and of one mind. With the entrance of the Gentiles differences of opinion arose, but not with the teaching authority. We have seen Peter and Paul acting in the same way towards them; and the other Apostles sent to pagan countries received their converts without subjecting them to any Jewish rites.

Some of the Jewish converts in Judea clung to the idea that the rite of circumcision was a necessary condition to salvation; they even came into Paul's field, and as the Acts tell us (XV.2) Paul and Barnabas "had no small contest with them." The question under discussion was so important that it demanded an immediate and definite solution. In appearance Paul seemed to dissent from the other Apostles.

The first Christians had for a few years the twelve Apostles with them, and it seems surprising that a similar question could arise. It concerned all future generations up to the end of time. Paul's arguments had not convinced the emissaries from Judea, who tenaciously clung to the Jewish traditions. The Christians at Antioch finally decided that Paul and Barnabas and some of the other side should go to Jerusalem, to the Apostles and priests and settle the question. The delegates were well received by the Church in Jerusalem, by the Apostles, and by the ancients. Besides the delegation Paul had also a special revelation concerning his journey to Jerusalem, as he himself informs us (Gal. II.1). At that time, as we learn from the same source (II.9) there were three Apostles in Jerusalem—James, Peter and John, the others were too far away. John was called from Ephesus, and Peter after his expulsion from Rome by Claudius, had returned to the mother church; James was Bishop of Jerusalem. At the meeting were present also the ancients or priests, that is, the priests of the first order or bishops as judges, and priests non-bishops who acted as advisors. We give to this meeting the name of Council, because it gave form to all ecclesiastical deliberative assemblies of the future, concerning the presidency, the freedom of discussion, and the right of bishops to express their opinion.

St. Paul, appointed an Apostle by Christ Himself, was not an inferior to the other Apostles, but his equality was not admitted by all and met with opposition. His work among the Gentiles could not but excite universal admiration. Peter had been the first to receive publicly a gentile into the Church, and had satisfactorily explained the justice of his act to the Church in Jerusalem. But when Paul began bringing them in en masse, the matter did not proceed so smoothly. Some false brethren thought they had too many arguments in their favor not to force upon pagan converts the Jewish rite of circumcision, before their admission into the Church. Christ had always conformed his life to the law; His teaching on that question was not understood by all in the same way. We need not wonder therefore that there was no uniform explicit belief about it. Hence the necessity to discuss the matter, to express personal appreciation of Christ's teaching, and above all to submit it to those, whom He had appointed guardians of His teaching. All the above circumstances led to the celebration of the Council of Jerusalem.

Paul and Barnabas began by relating the great things God had done through their ministry among the Gentiles. This was the logical way to bring the question before the assembly. They told the Council that some converted Pharisees had arisen, and insisted that the pagan converts must be circumcised, and be commanded to observe the law of Moses (XV.5).

The question was freely and fully discussed. After that, Peter, as chief of the Apostles and supreme visible head of the Church, rose to settle the dispute. He decided that the Gentiles can be received into the Church without circumcision, and he gave the following reasons for his decision: 1. God had so declared by a revelation (7). 2. He confirmed it by pouring forth the Holy Ghost upon them (v. 8). 3. The Gentiles are no longer impure, because they had been purified through faith (v. 9). 4. An intolerable burden would be put upon them (v. 10). 5. Salvation must be obtained through the grace of Christ, not through the observance of the law (v. 11). Paul added the signs and wonders, which God had wrought among the Gentiles (v. 12). James confirmed it by the prophet Amos (v. 15).

Peter's discourse was very short and simple. The silence of the assembly approved his every word. Paul and Barnabas approved Peter's decision by referring to the wonderful ways of God in their work among the Gentiles. The last of the speakers was James, one of the Apostles, and bishop of Jerusalem. He may have been looked upon by the opponents of Paul, as one likely to side with them. In later centuries some have claimed superiority for him in the presidency of the Council. Their arguments are that when Paul in his letter to the Galatians (II.9) writes of the three Apostles present at the Council, he mentions James first, and that at the meeting he is the last speaker.   The reason why Paul mentions James first probably was that in an effort to win his opponents, he gave first place to one, who seemed more in favor with them.   Peter had already expressed himself on the question, when he gave an account of the conversion of Cornelius.   He, however, settled the question of faith concerning the requirements of the law as means of salvation.   James adds his approval to the decision, and further requests that a few points of discipline be suggested to the Gentile converts, in order to promote the right understanding between all classes to be gathered into the one church —Jew and Gentile.   These suggestions were adopted by the Council.

These suggestions were the following: 1. That the Gentiles refrain from the pollution of idols, that is, from the flesh of victims immolated to false gods; the eating savored of idolatry and the Mosaic law strongly condemned it (Ex. XXXIV.15).   2. That they abstain from fornication.   Morals at that time were so low among the Gentiles, that simple fornication was looked upon as something indifferent.   3. That they abstain from things strangled.   The chief motive of this prohibition was that the Jews abhorred these things; to avoid friction with the Jews, the Gentiles were ordered to submit to that prescription of the Old Law.   This order was given, not because the law of Moses still prevailed and was to be imposed on the Gentiles, but because the Apostles made a new disciplinary law of it to procure the spirit of good fellowship between the Jews and the Gentiles.

Peter and James had both declared that the law and the legal prescriptions were no longer binding on the Christians.   4. That they abstain from blood, in order not to resemble in any way the barbarians of that time.

All these prohibitions, with the exception of fornication, which is always sinful, slowly disappeared, when Jewish and Gentile converts were so united that there was no longer any need for them.   To please his Jewish converts James added that there was no need for Christians to honor Moses, as he was sufficiently honored by the Jews in their synagogues.

The decrees of the Council were written and promulgated by the Apostles and by the seniors, that is, by the bishops, not by the faithful.   The teaching Church had pronounced sentence; it issued the decrees.   The beginning words of the decree are: "It hath seemed good to the Holy Ghost and to us" (XV.28).   The definition is one of faith and morals. In framing it, the teaching body, that is, the Apostles and the Bishops, not only claim the assistance of the Holy Ghost, but ascribe the decision to the Holy Ghost, like to themselves.   The teaching Church was convinced of its unerring knowledge in defining questions of that kind.   In their letter of promulgation the Apostles called the suggestions of James necessary things.   With the exception of fornication, they are not so in themselves, but on account of circumstances. As soon as circumstances permitted, that disciplinary law was abrogated.

The decree of the Council was disciplinary rather

than dogmatic; particular, not universal; transitory, not permanent. The only point of discussion was whether the law of Moses concerning circumcision should be enforced on the Gentiles or not. The Council decided that it should not, but it did not decide whether the law of Moses was still binding on the Jewish converts or not; that question had not been raised. The suggestions of James seem to indicate that they thought so. This explains the incident at Antioch, where Peter endeavored to satisfy both parties and drew upon himself the sharp rebuke of Paul. We have seen that Peter and Paul acted in the same way on former occasions, and that their faith was absolutely identical. The little controversy served to draw closer the bonds of affection between the two great teachers of the Church, crowning it with martyrdom in the same city on the same day.

The Council sent two messengers—Judas and Silas —to accompany Paul and Barnabas on their return, in order to convince fully the Gentiles that the views of Paul on these questions were those of the other Apostles and of the Seniors. The Council of Jerusalem was the first gathering of the teaching body of the Church; it is the pattern, after which all similar gatherings have been modelled.

CHAPTER EIGHTEENTH

On their return to Antioch, Paul and Barnabas with the two messengers, delivered the letter of the Council to the multitude. Great joy and consolation prevailed on the reading of it. Judas and Silas, as they were prophets in the broad sense, that is, under divine inspiration were endowed with holy and efficacious wisdom, contributed not a little to the general satisfaction, and confirmed the brethren in the faith. After spending some time in Antioch, the messengers were let go with the best wishes of the community. Silas, however, decided to remain. Paul and Barnabas continued teaching and evangelizing for some days; the Acts do not state how many. It was during those days after the Council of Jerusalem, that Peter arrived at Antioch, and Paul administered that public rebuke, of which he speaks in his letter to the Galatians (II.11), and of which we treated in chapter second. After that Paul suggested to Barnabas that they visit again the same places, which they had covered during their first tour. Barnabas agreed, but desired to take along John Mark, his nephew. Paul was of a different opinion and argued that John Mark should not be accepted as a companion, because he had deserted them once before in Pamphylia. Paul and Barnabas were both holy men, but that did not prevent an occasional disagreement between them; they did not always view all things in the same light. On this occasion they thought better to part company; Paul and Silas went their own way; Barnabas and Mark sailed for Cyprus. God drew good from the dissension or the imperfection of His Apostles for the speedier propagation of the Gospel. The dissension, however, did not last very long; after a few years they were together again, as we read in Paul's first epistle to the Corinthians (IX.6); even John Mark later joined Paul (Col. IV.10–11).

Paul left accompanied by Silas and with the best wishes of the Christians of Antioch, who seem to have sided with him in his recent controversy with Peter. This time they traveled by land, not by sea. They visited Syria and Cilicia; they knew that it was not enough to convert but that proper care must be taken of the converts; they insist this time upon the observance, not only of the commandments of God, but also of the precepts given by men, such as the Apostles and the Seniors. Paul went to Derbe and Lystra, where the first remarkable incident occurred as related in the Acts.

Timothy was most probably a Lystrian, converted together with his mother to the faith at Paul's first visit. The Acts give some details concerning this favorite disciple of St. Paul. His father was a Gentile and his mother a Jewess. Such a convert was a suitable companion of Paul on his apostolic peregrinations. About 11 or 12 years later he was the recipient of two letters from the great Apostle. These give us an insight of the cordial relations that existed between them.

The Jews had been forbidden to marry Canaanite women, but that prohibition did not include other Gentile women. Scripture gives us several instances of such marriages. Jacob, Joseph, and Moses married heathen women. Esther married the heathen, Assuerus. In the beginning of the Church the Christians often married heathens. In later years such marriages were forbidden by the Church, to which alone Christ had given power to regulate the contract, which He had raised to the dignity of a sacrament.

The Christians of Lystra and Iconium entertained the most favorable opinion of Timothy, and so had expressed it to the Apostle. Paul circumcised him, not because the law made it obligatory; the Council of Jerusalem at which Paul had assisted had declared it unnecessary, but because he desired to yield as far as he could in order to gain all. Timothy was to be his companion, and the Jews certainly would not take a change of religion, nor hear of the coming of the Messiah from one who was not even a Jew. The controversy that brought about the Council of Jerusalem had never divided the judeo- and pagano-Christians in those places. There was no fear therefore in submitting willing Timothy to that Jewish rite. On another occasion when defence of the truth demanded it, Paul absolutely refused to have his disciple Titus submit to it at Jerusalem, and he openly rebuked Peter for favoring the Jews on that account. A few years later, in his letter to the Galatians (V.2), he openly condemned circumcision.

After passing through Phrygia and Galatia, they intended to go to what was then called Asia. Asia was then a Roman province comprising the western part of Asia Minor, adjacent to the Egean sea. Ephesus was the capital of that province. They were on their way to it, when they were forbidden by the Holy Ghost to preach the Gospel in Asia (Acts XVI.6) at least for the present. Through Phrygia they went east to Galatia to preach the Gospel. Then they crossed Galatia from east to west into Mysia, which was part of the forbidden territory, with the intention of going north into Bithynia, but again the Spirit of Jesus, that is, the Holy Ghost who proceeds from the Father and of the Son, forbade them. On the strength of this prohibition they had no alternative but to retrace their steps or go west. They crossed Mysia and came to the seaboard town of Troas, perhaps with the intention of returning by water to Antioch of Syria. Troas was at that time a port of great importance for the trade between Asia Minor and Macedonia. This town was not far away from ancient Troas, made famous by the songs of Homer. Uncertain as to what course to follow, Paul had a vision during the night. An angel in the human form of a Macedonian stood before him, and besought him to pass over into Macedonia and to help his countrymen. This was a sufficient indication to

Paul that God's will demanded his presence there, and he immediately devised means to carry it out. They were now four in the party—Paul, Luke, Silas, and Timothy. They sailed in a straight northern course to Neapolis and Philippi in Thrace. That part of Macedonia, of which Philippi was the first city, was a Roman colony. The various colonies of Rome served as an outlet for its surplus population, as a help to the poor, among whom they divided the unoccupied land. The colonies also offered an opportunity for a military career, as soldiers were sent to them to protect Roman rights. Apparently in this city there was no synagogue. When the Jews were forbidden to have a meeting place within a city, they built an oratory on the banks of a river or on the seashore, so as to have water for the legal ablutions.

On the Sabbath day the missionaries went forth without the gate by a river side, where they noticed a number of women meeting for prayer; they sat down among them and began to speak to them. The Acts mention one of these women by name—Lydia. She came from Thyatira, and was a seller of purple, that is, of wool or of cloth dyed in purple; the art of dyeing was peculiar to her native land. She worshipped the true God and took to heart the words of Paul. After she and her household with her had been baptized, Lydia entreated the missionaries to accept the hospitality of her house; they accepted.

The Acts here relate an incident which shows that there is nothing new under the sun. Soothsayers and

Spiritists were not unknown in those days; then like now there were people who for a pecuniary consideration availed themselves of poor fallen creatures. At Philippi there was a girl with a pythonical spirit, one who reveals the future and the occult. A python was an enormous snake, which in the mythology of the day was killed by Apollo, the god of divination. This girl followed Paul and his companions when they were on their way to prayer and cried out: "These men are the servants of the Most High, who preach unto you the way of salvation" (XVI.17). She did this for many days. The soothsayer in this case certainly told the truth, but Paul had no misgivings as to what the spirit was that caused her so to speak, and that possessed her. He was no other than the devil. Paul would not be praised by a lying and impure spirit, and was grieved over the condition of the poor girl. He commanded in the name of Jesus Christ the devil to go out of her and he did so immediately. All were not pleased with this miracle. The masters of the poor girl, on seeing a great source of income gone, were not slow in taking revenge. They apprehended Paul and Silas and brought them into the marketplace before the magistrates. History does not tell us why Luke and Timothy were not apprehended at the same time. The complaint was that those men, because they were Jews, disturbed the city. The Romans and the other Gentiles hated the Jews because of their peculiarities in faith and morals; they hated the Christians, because they were originally Jews. The Apostle was preaching a

God, who had not been added to the list of gods by decree of the Roman senate; in that manner only could new gods be created. Tiberius Cæsar after hearing of the miracles of Christ wished to find a place for Him among the Roman gods, but the senate refused because they had not been consulted first of all.

Paul and Silas were indeed guilty of the imaginary offence; the sentence was a flogging and imprisonment. The scourging had covered them with stripes; they were then cast into prison and the jailer was instructed to guard them diligently. To prevent a possible escape he thrust them into an inner prison, and made their feet fast in the stocks. Stocks were wooden boards with two openings, into which the feet of the prisoners were forced. At midnight while Paul was praying and thanking God aloud for the indignities heaped upon them, to the hearing of prisoners and jailers, a tremendous earthquake shook the very foundations of the prison; all the doors were thrown open, and the bands of all prisoners were loosed. God again showed that all the elements are subject to his bidding, and must contribute to the fulfilment of Paul's mission. The jailer, thinking that his prisoners had escaped, was about to kill himself in despair, when Paul cried out to him with a loud voice: "Do thyself no harm, for we all are here." The jailer went in, fell down at the feet of Paul and Silas, and brought them out. He then asked them: "Masters, what must I do, that I may be saved?" (XVI.30). The earthquake was the occasion for the conversion of the jailer; he saw in it the hand of God protecting His Apostles. Paul immediately gave him and his household the necessary instruction and baptized them. The jailer had washed the wounds of the two Apostles, and laid the table for them; there was great rejoicing in the house.

When morning came, the magistrates sent the sergeants to release the men, but Paul was not prepared to recover his freedom in that way; he wanted justice done. He insisted that, as the magistrates had condemned them without a hearing, they themselves should come to release them. The magistrates well knew that they had violated the Valerian and the Porcian law, which forbade to scourge a Roman citizen. A lawful procedure had to be followed, and before the infliction of such punishment, a Roman citizen, if the case demanded it, had to be convicted and deprived of his rights. One guilty of scourging a Roman citizen without that procedure was guilty of the crime of lese majesty against the Roman people; his case was dealt with in Rome and the death sentence was imposed. Both Paul and Silas claimed to be Roman citizens; their claim was not contested; all knew that a false claim was punishable with death. According to the inspired narrative, Paul and Silas returned to the prison, after they had dined at the house of the converted jailer. After the magistrates realized that they had overstepped their rights in the treatment of a Roman citizen, they were seized with a dreadful fear, and entreated the prisoners to come out and leave the city. Paul did not appeal to the Roman authorities, but left the prison, went to the house of Lydia to comfort the Christians, especially Luke and Timothy, and then quietly left the town.

The four missionaries proceeded west through Amphipolis and Apollonia to Thessalonica. This city had a synagogue; the fact proves that there was a goodly number of Jews. For three Sabbaths Paul went to the synagogue and explained the Scriptures. He proved that Jesus, whom he preached, was the Christ who according to the prophecies was to die and rise again. Some of the Jews believed and joined Paul and Silas; many of the Godfearing Hellenists were converted and not a few noble women (XVII.4).

The Jews filled with envy stirred up a persecution against them; they got the loafers and the worst elements in the city to join them in a riotous uproar. They went to the house of Jason, whose hospitality Paul and Silas had accepted, and insisted that he give up the two men, with the avowed intention of illtreating them. The guests were not there; in their stead they seized Jason and some Christians, and dragged them before the rulers of the city, and threw the blame for the commotion on them. Jason was covering men who had proclaimed another king against the orders of Cæsar; this other king was no other than Jesus. They compelled Jason to swear allegiance to the Roman Empire and to Cæsar, and to be a bondman for Paul; Jason would be responsible if Paul were found guilty. It was an easy task for Jason to prove that Paul had no evil intentions against the empire; the prisoners were set free.   Under the circumstances Paul and Silas thought it best to leave the city; during the night they went to Berea.

However badly Paul had been treated on several occasions by the Jews, in Berea he went again with Silas to the synagogue.   Persecution did not frighten him; on the contrary it seems to make him all the more anxious to procure their eternal salvation.   In Berea Paul had to deal with people of nobler sentiments.   They eagerly listened to him, and they found by the daily reading of the Bible that Paul's teaching perfectly conformed to the prophecies of the Old Testament concerning the Messiah.   They examined the new faith with the light they had, before they embraced it.   Many men and honorable pagan women were added to the Church.   The Jews at Thessalonica had meanwhile heard of the grand success of Paul in Berea, and they tried again their previous trick.   They came over, stirred up and troubled the multitude.   Paul and the converted brethren thought prudent for him to avoid the snares set him by his enemies.   He left Silas and Timothy to perfect the religious instruction of the neophytes, and proceeded towards the sea.   Those who had conducted Paul thus far, sailed with him to Athens, the intellectual, scientific and artistic capital of the world, as Rome was the political capital.   The Bereans then returned to their city with a message from the Apostle to Silas and Timothy to follow him immediately.

CHAPTER NINETEENTH

PAUL AT ATHENS AND AT CORINTH

PAUL's original plan was not to go so far west as Athens; he had been called to Macedonia only (Acts XVI.9). A combination of circumstances almost against his will, brought him to the capital of Greece, the mother of arts and of philosophy. Athens was to be the scene of a contest between human and divine wisdom. Athens had within its borders a multitude of poets, orators, and philosophers. Their poems and discourses in honor of the gods prove that Paul was quite correct in his appreciation of the idolatrous city. Athens in this regard excelled all other cities of the empire, and for the number of its gods and altars it held first place among the cities of Greece. The field which Paul was going to cultivate differed greatly from all other places where he had preached the word of God. Elsewhere he had spoken either to Jews who expected the Messiah, or to simple and ignorant heathens. We find him now in the midst of proud philosophers, in a city of the highest culture, superficial though it was. Paul's spirit was stirred within him, seeing the city wholly given to idolatry (XVII.16). Paul did not exaggerate. Pausanias before him thought that there were more gods in

Athens than in the rest of the world. Petronius claimed that it was easier to find a god than a man. The harvest offered the brightest prospects; Paul therefore insisted that his co-workers, Silas and Timothy, join him immediately. He began by disputing with the Jews in their synagogue, and with the others who served God, but these were probably few in number. Then he was to be seen every day in the marketplace, where he found a larger audience, because there the philosophers and the orators addressed the people.

His first argument was with the Epicureans and the Stoics, as we learn from the Acts (XVII.18). Athens had at that time, besides these, two other schools of philosophy following the renowned Plato and Aristotle. The first two denied the immortality of the soul. As Paul preached the resurrection of the dead, it is possible that only these took part in the argument. Epicurus taught that man's supreme happiness consisted in sensual pleasure, which theory Horace called a pig from Epicurus' herd. Pagan writers have left us several details of his licentious life. He is said to be the author of the saying: Eat, drink, and play, after death there is no pleasure. Paul had learned in his youth that his fellow-citizens of Tarsus carried out that motto.

The Stoics, severe and morose, were the opposite of the Epicureans; Zeno was their founder. The chief tenets of the Stoics were the following: God is fate; all things are ruled by fate; virtue consists in the power and the industry of the individual; all virtues are alike as are also all vices, he who has one has them all; no pity and no mercy to the culprit, because these dispositions are weaknesses of the mind; a wise man may have to end his own life; all gods, except Jupiter are mortal and eventually will be transformed into Jupiter; God is the soul of the world; he therefore goes under different names according to the objects which he animates—Neptune of the sea, Ceres of the land, Bacchus of the vine, etc.

Both the Epicureans and the Stoics were polytheists, or rather atheists; admitting many gods is denying the one true God.   Throughout the history of the Church the voluptuous Epicureans and the arrogant Stoics will prove to be its worst enemies.   With such theories Paul had to contend.   He had to show his hearers that virtue, goodness, and salvation can only be found in the crucified Christ, by whose grace and power we may be raised to eternal life, that He is the mediator between God and man, that his life chaste, pious, and holy must be the norm of our life.

Some of Paul's hearers thought that there was no sense in all he prated; others were of the opinion that, as he preached to them Jesus and the Resurrection, he was endeavoring to introduce new gods.   They took him up to Mars hill, or to the Areopagus, where far removed from the noise of the market place he could explain to the curious Athenians what he meant by the new things he had brought to their ears (XVII.20).   The supreme court used to meet here and the name Areopagus was also applied to it, but Paul was not dragged before judges; he does not say a word in his own defence; he had simply accepted a polite invitation. The author of the Acts incidentally remarks that the Athenians did so, not for love of the truth, but out of vain curiosity. Plutarch and others show up, as does Luke, the garrulous curiosity of the Athenians; they had always time to hear the latest and always looked for new surprises; the market place and the barber shop were the information bureaus.

Paul had come to them with something entirely new; they were anxious to hear him in the vast Areopagus. Paul standing in the center began his discourse by praising them in order to captivate their benevolence: "Ye men of Athens, I perceive that in all things you are too superstitious" (XVII.22). To praise them he uses an ambiguous term; he praises their religious dispositions, but insinuates that these are not the worship of the true God; he calls them superstitious, that is, over religious; he did not wish to offend nor to flatter.

On his wanderings through the city Paul had seen their idols. An altar dedicated to an unknown God had especially struck his attention, and formed the basis of his discourse; he was the God whom Paul announced. The Athenians worshipped that God in their ignorance; they thought him to be a god like Jupiter or Minerva. They implicitly worshipped the true God without knowing Him explicitly. Paul was addressing heathens and therefore did not call him the God of Abraham and Isaac, as he did on former occasions in his meetings with the Jews. He was speaking to philosophers, and therefore described God in a philosophical way, so as to make it plain that He is the only God, and that all other gods are false. He first showed Him to be the Creator of all, which the Epicureans denied; no pagan philosopher ever had a clearer conception of creation. He then proceeded to show that He was the Lord and Ruler of the whole world, while the gods of the heathens were national and local, that therefore He cannot be enclosed in handmade temples, and that the heathens act wrongly in offering food and drink to support Him, as He gives life to all. He taught them that all mankind proceeded from one couple, that God distributed the earth among them and appointed times and limits, and that God's providence ruled all and everything. This upset the theory of the Stoics and other pagans, to whom Fate was the only explanation of the world's phenomena. Incidentally Paul made them understand the unity of the human race, which polytheism did not admit. Idolatry divided the nations; each one had its own gods; their myths assigned a different origin to the various peoples and caused hatred among them.

In explaining how in God we live, and move and are (XVII.28) he did not quote from the Scriptures, as he would have done in addressing Jews, but appealed to the testimony of their own poets—Aratus and others, who said: For we are also his offspring, that is, of Jupiter. Paul applied this but in different manner to the true God. Finally he alluded to Christ and His resurrection from the dead, and insisted upon the necessity of penance and of giving up the worship of idols.

When hearing of the resurrection of the dead, some mocked him, probably the Epicureans; others probably Stoics said: "We will hear thee again about this matter" (32). The Athenians were lightheaded and proud, two moral dispositions that prevent the word of God from sprouting and bringing forth fruit. Yet the sacred writer assures us that Paul's efforts were not in vain; he had made some notable converts, such as Denis the Areopagite and a woman named Domaris. Denis was one of the most famous of the judges of the Areopagus, and he was afterwards appointed by the Apostle bishop of Athens. He left us some very sublime books on such subjects as: The celestial and ecclesiastical hierarchy, mystic theology, etc. The church of Athens flourished wonderfully during his episcopate. The great cause or occasion of Denis' conversion was the miraculous darkening of the sun at the death of Christ, when at Heliopolis in Egypt he in wonderment exclaimed: "Either the God of nature suffers or this world will be destroyed." The suffering God was the unknown God, of whom Paul spoke and in whom Denis believed. After his conversion he followed the Apostle for a few years to perfect his religious education, and then went with him to Jerusalem, where he was present, as he himself attests, at the death and burial of Christ's Mother. He wrote a letter to St. John in exile at Patmos and foretold to him a speedy return. Shortly afterwards St. John advised him to go to Rome to see Clement, the third successor of Peter. Clement sent him with Rusticus and Eleutherius to Gaul to preach the Gospel. As bishop of Paris in extreme old age he was beheaded for the faith. A constant tradition, accepted by the best critics, holds that after being beheaded he carried his head in his hands and walked two miles; the angels furnished the triumphal music.

Paul left Athens and proceeded to Corinth. Here he met a Jew named Aquila, and his wife Priscilla, who had recently come over from Italy, owing to the expulsion of the Jews from Rome by order of Claudius. Suetonius tells us that for continuous uproars under the leadership of Chrestus, Claudius expelled the Jews from Rome; so does the pagan author confirm the account given by the inspired writer.

That edict must have soon fallen into desuetude, because a few years later we again find Aquila and Priscilla in Rome (Rom. XVI.3). Aquila was a tentmaker like Paul; the Apostle accepted his hospitality and worked with him. As usual he went every Sabbath to the synagogue and preached Jesus to both Jews and Greeks; he preached on the Sabbath and worked during the week, so as not to be a burden to any one. When Silas and Timothy joined him from Macedonia, he devoted all his time to the preaching of God's word. We know from the letters of Paul that these two disciples were with him in Athens, whence he sent them back to Thessalonica and remained alone (1 Thes. III.1–2). From his second letter to the Corinthians (XI.8–9) we may

conclude that Silas and Timothy brought to Paul
help in money, which the liberal Philippians had contributed to his support.   For that reason Paul was
enabled to devote himself to preaching without being compelled to do handwork.   So far the chief at-
tentions of Paul were for the Jews, but they gainsaid
him and blasphemed Christ.   In holy anger he shook
his garments and told them: "Your blood be upon
your own heads; I am clean; from henceforth I will
go unto the Gentiles" (XVIII.6).   Paul had done his
duty; they were to blame for their continued blindness; they were their own murderers.

Leaving the synagogue, he went to the neighboring house of Titus the Just, a man who worshipped
God; there he continued to preach the Gospel, thereby
giving an opportunity to the Jews to hear him, if they
wished.   Whether he changed his residence is not
said, but he certainly kept up friendly relations with
Aquila and Priscilla.   The sentiments that had been
expressed by the Jews seemed to preclude the possibility of their conversion, but a conversion is the
work of God's grace.   Paul soon numbered among
his converts some very prominent Jews.   Among
them was the ruler of the synagogue—Crispus with
all his house.   We know from his first epistle to the
Corinthians (I.14) that he baptized with his own
hand Crispus, Caius, and the household of Stephen;
but many others had been baptized, probably by
Silas and Timothy.

Paul had occasion to fear that after the conversion
of its ruler the whole synagogue would turn against

him. He had a vision during the night. The Lord bade him not to fear, but to speak and not to hold his peace; He promised that he would not be hurt and that a rich harvest of souls awaited him (XVIII.9–10). Paul remained in Corinth one year and six months. Gallio was for that last year proconsul of Achaia; he was the brother of Seneca, Nero's teacher. Nero himself was Claudius' stepson and had been adopted as a son by the emperor. It is possible that Paul made the acquaintance of Seneca; some have claimed that there was even an exchange of letters between them. It is certain, however, that Seneca did not become a Christian, but lived and died a Stoic.

The Jews again rose up against Paul with one accord, and brought him before the judgment seat of Gallio. They accused him of persuading men to worship God contrary to law, both of the Jews and of the Romans. The Jewish law forbade to worship a corporeal God, and the Roman law forbade the admission of new gods without a decree of the Senate. Gallio held that this Roman law applied to Rome only and not to the provinces; he did not take the Jewish law into consideration at all. As there was no question of a crime, such as theft or murder, he did not think that religious matters were of his competence, and he refused to be a judge of such things. He drove them all away from the judgment seat. Having failed to impress the proconsul with their tale, they turned their anger on the ruler of the synagogue—Sosthenes, the successor of Crispus, who had previously been converted by Paul. Sosthenes was a Christian at heart and favored the Apostle. In the eyes of the Jews he was a traitor, who had lost their case and they beat him before the judgment seat. Gallio cared not for what happened; fear of drawing their anger upon his head prevented him from protecting the innocence of Sosthenes and the peace of the empire. Paul was not in the least upset by recent occurrences, and fearlessly protracted his stay for several days.

At this point the sacred writer informs us that Paul had shorn his head, for he had a vow (XVIII.18). He shore his head, either because he had formerly taken the vow of the Nazarites, or a similar vow that no scissor or razor should touch his head and that time had expired, or more probably because he wished to offer the Eucharistic sacrifice in the temple, and therefore abstained for the thirty days previous from wine, and cut his hair. Josephus Flavius informs us that such a custom prevailed among the Jews. The first alternative is hardly possible, because the vow of the Nazarites (Numbers VI) demanded that the head be shaved in Jerusalem before the Tabernacle, and the hair be burned as a sacrifice.

Paul left Corinth in his own good time with Aquila and Priscilla and went to Ephesus, where he left them, probably to prepare his way. Ephesus was the metropolis of Asia Minor; it possessed the famous temple of Diana, and a multitude of orators and philosophers. St. John frequently resided there, when he founded and ruled the churches of Asia. According to tradition the Blessed Mother of Jesus was there cared for by St. John for some years. Although requested to tarry a longer time, Paul would not consent, but promised to return if it was God's will; he intended now to celebrate the approaching feast in Jerusalem.

Paul went down to Cesarea and thence to Jerusalem, where he probably met the Mother of God, to whom he related his trials and whose patronage he implored. He made only a short stay in the Holy City, and returned to Antioch, the city he loved so well. This completed the second apostolic journey of St. Paul.

At this point in the sacred history of the Church the inspired writer abruptly intercepts the work of the great Apostle to acquaint us with another agency for the propagation of Christianity in the early days; we mean the lay apostolate. Three such lay apostles are set as models before us—Aquila, Priscilla, and Apollo. We have had occasion to mention the services of the first two; Appollo now enters upon the scene. He was a Jew, born at Alexandria, and praised for his eloquence and his knowledge of the Scriptures. His religion was apparently a surprising mixture. In his fervor he spoke accurately of Jesus, and at the same time knew only the Baptism of John. How could that happen? He must have learned from John the Baptist or from his disciples that Jesus of Nazareth was the Messiah promised to the Jews, and that the baptism of penance was necessary.   Although only a catechumen he began to speak boldly in the synagogue, while his own spiritual instruction was being perfected by the two lay workers—Priscilla and Aquila.   The wife here is mentioned before the husband to show that she had the larger share in the Christian education of Apollo. Eloquent and well versed in the Scriptures Apollo submits with humility and docility to the teaching of Priscilla and Aquila.   We find in the first epistle to the Corinthians (III.6) Paul's sentiments concerning this lay apostolate.   He places the work of Apollo on a level with his own; "I have planted, Apollo watered, but God gave the increase."   All the early Christians, although not with equal prominence, endeavored to make Jesus known to their fellow men. Brotherly love was the Master's own command; the early Christians knew that the best proof of that love was their coöperation with Christ for the salvation of the world.

CHAPTER TWENTIETH

AFTER Paul had paid a visit to Jerusalem, he returned to Ephesus according to his promise. His stay in Ephesus gives us a clear insight into the dogmatic and disciplinary teaching of the primitive Church. On his arrival Paul found some disciples, who had never heard of the Holy Ghost; they had been baptized in John's baptism. Who were these? They could not have been baptized and instructed by Apollo, or Aquila or Priscilla, for in that case they would have known that the baptism of John had been superseded by that of Christ. They either had been baptized by John some twenty years before, when on a visit to Jerusalem for the holidays, or they had recently come from some part of Judea, where the Christian religion had not been preached. From the question put to them by Paul: In what then were you baptized? the conclusion seems evident that in those days Baptism was conferred with the express mention of the Holy Ghost, not in the mere name of Christ. After Paul had explained the necessity of Christian baptism those disciples were baptized.

He then imposed his hands upon them and the Holy Ghost came down upon them, and they spoke with tongues and prophesied (XIX.8). This is the same rite which we saw Peter and John conferring on the converts of Philip in Samaria after their baptism, and with the same results. This rite was entirely distinct from baptism, and was called in later years Confirmation. There were about twelve men so confirmed.

For three months in succession Paul continued to teach in the synagogue; with what results the Acts do not state, but some were hardened, and not only refused to obey, but even cursed the way of the Lord before the multitude. Paul left them to their reprobate sense and for the next two years he continued his missionary labors in the school of one Tyrannus, or of a certain tyrant. It is not certain whether this was the proper name of an individual, or the common name for a powerful man, a ruler of possibly royal descent. For school we may probably understand the porch of the house. The reasons why Paul selected this place are not given in the Acts; perhaps to have the protection of a powerful man against the audacity of the Jews. During those two years most of the people of Asia, both Jews and Gentiles, had an opportunity to hear the word of God; the Jews were attracted to Ephesus by business motives, and the Gentiles to worship in the famous temple of Diana.

At this period of the history of the Church the Acts inform us that God wrought more than ordinary miracles by the hand of Paul. Handkerchiefs and aprons that had been used by the Apostles were eagerly sought, and applied to the sick and the possessed, with the result that diseases departed from them, and that the wicked spirits were driven out. God by working the miracles evidently approved the practice.

As the magicians of Pharaoh endeavored to offset or duplicate the miracles of Moses, so some of the Jewish exorcists tried to drive out the evil spirits by adopting the formula of Paul; viz., in the name of the Lord Jesus. The seven sons of the Jewish rabbi, Sceva, tried it, but the evil spirits knew the difference, and exclaimed: "Jesus I know, Paul I know, but who are you?" (XIX.15.) The evil spirit leaped upon two of Sceva's sons and mastered them, until they fled out of that house naked and wounded. They thought that words on the lips of Paul would have the same efficacy on their own, but they soon learned their mistake. The Jewish Church before Christ had its exorcists; and so long as it was the true church, it had power to cast out devils in the name of Jehovah; but God was no longer with it. The devil had the best of these last supposed exorcists. Their failure soon became known to Jews and Gentiles; fear fell upon them all to the greater honor of the name of Jesus.

The Acts give us the proof that the above occurrence had made a deep impression. Of the believers many came to confess and declare their sins. We need not necessarily believe that here for the first time we meet with auricular confession; it may have been a general and public confession. The Gentiles

who had been converted through the failure of
Sceva's sons, were preparing for baptism and acted
as the believers. Many of them gave a most interesting proof of their sincerity, that calls for followers
even in the present day. Those who had followed
curious arts, brought together their books on magic
and burnt them. To show the extent of these practices in Ephesus and at the same time of the sacrifice
they made preparatory to their admission in the
Church, the Acts expressly record that an appraise-
ment was made and that the value of books so burnt
represented in value about seven thousand dollars of
our currency.

Paul meanwhile was thinking of his trip to Jerusalem, and was on his way to visit Macedonia and
Achaia, and then the inspired writer makes him say:
"After I have been there, I must see Rome also"
(XIX.21). His first intention was to go from Ephesus to Corinth, then proceed into Macedonia, return
thence to Corinth, and then go to Jerusalem. He
changed his plan somewhat so as to avoid Corinth
(2 Cor. I.15–16). He did not wish to see them in
sorrow, but to spare them he desires them first to
amend their ways, which he hoped would be the result of his first epistle, and also of the warnings of
Timothy, whom he soon after sent to them. Paul's
ardent desire of seeing Rome was more in the nature
of an interior impulse of the Holy Ghost; he wished
to give some help to the Church founded by Peter,
but his wish was not granted immediately; four long

years would pass, two of which in prison, and then he would go, not as a free Roman, but as a prisoner under military escort.

Paul sent two of his helpers—Timothy and Evastus—into Macedonia, to prepare the ways for his coming, and especially to arrange for the collection in favor of the poor Christians of Jerusalem. He further determined that Timothy should go from Macedonia to Corinth, and try to settle the disagreements, that had arisen in that Church. Shortly before messengers had come to advise Paul of grave dissensions at Corinth. He then wrote his first epistle to the Corinthians. It reached its destination before Timothy's arrival in that city. Paul's intention was to tarry at Ephesus until Pentecost, for a great door and evident was opened to him, that is, there was hope of many conversions; but at the same time he had many adversaries (1 Cor. XVI. 8.9).

Meanwhile Paul's work at Ephesus had aroused the anger of a certain class of citizens. This led to a great disturbance similar to the one at Philippi (XVI). It was not an explosion on the part of the Jews or of fanaticism, but the immediate cause of it was a pecuniary consideration of one of the crafts. Paul's preaching was affecting adversely the trade of the silversmiths. He had drawn away by persuasion a great multitude of the city and of all Asia from the worship of the great Diana of the Ephesians; the silversmiths were the losers. Their chief product was copies in silver of the temple of Diana, with a statuette of the goddess inside. The temple of Diana at that time was mentioned as one of the seven wonders of the world; it contained a statue of Diana, which the Ephesians believed had come down from heaven. The copies were in great demand and had a ready sale. Demetrius was probably the foreman of the craft; he was not slow in foreseeing that if secessions continued at the same rate, their trade was in danger. He called the members of the craft together and explained to them that their trade and their gains were in danger of being destroyed, and that even the temple of Diana would be reputed for nothing. After hearing this statement, all shouted: Great is Diana of the Ephesians! The whole city was filled with confusion (XIX.2-9). Instead of going for Paul, the angry crowd seized hold of Gaius and Aristarchus, two of Paul's companions from Macedonia, and rushed them into the theatre, that is, the courtroom. Paul wished to throw himself immediately into the crowd, but his disciples, and some of his friends among the rulers of Asia, dissuaded him from doing so, while others called for him. Those called by the sacred writer rulers of Asia were ten men, who had charge of the public games and of the sacred ceremonies in honor of the gods and of the emperor. They were selected from among the influential men of the country; their office was not remunerated and entailed many expenses. As Paul had friends among them he certainly had acquired prestige with the upper class. Great confusion prevailed among the crowd in the courtroom; many did not know what had brought them there; they had followed the rush without being aware of the motive. There were many Jews among them. The silversmiths did not look with favor upon them; they knew that they had no respect for Diana, and therefore did not patronize them. The Jews selected one Alexander from among themselves to call the meeting to order. Their intention was to exculpate themselves by showing that they had nothing in common with the teaching of Paul. Alexander beckoned with his hand for silence, but when the audience realized that he was a Jew, pandemonium broke loose, and for two hours they kept shouting: Great is Diana of the Ephesians! Finally the town clerk succeeded in appeasing the multitude and Alexander was allowed to speak. The inspired writer has preserved for us at least a part of his speech, which for good logic appealed to the people. To ingratiate himself with his audience, Alexander began by telling them that the whole world knew their devotedness to the great Diana, Jupiter's offspring; then he requested them to be quiet and do nothing rashly. He added an officious lie by stating that the prisoners were not guilty of sacrilege, nor of blasphemy against the goddess. He finally advised the craftsmen that, if they had a case against any man, the courts of justice were open to them, and that for any other matter a lawful assembly may decide. He warned them further that they were in danger of having to give an account of that day's uproar; that they might be accused of sedition before the emperor or the proconsul. He concluded that there was no one to blame for the day's concourse and dismissed the assembly. It appears that all took the hint and quietly dispersed.

We must remark that here and elsewhere Luke omits to mention many and important facts; he touches only superficially upon some incidents in the travels of Paul. Paul says that he was scourged three times; only one scourging is mentioned. Not a word is said about Peter's episcopate in Antioch and in Rome. Paul writes about his fight with beasts at Ephesus (1 Cor. XV.32). Luke does not mention what happened in that regard. Did he mean that the Ephesians acted as beasts towards him, when he had far worse encounters with the Jews at Derbe, Lystra, and Corinth? and yet nowhere are they called beasts. It was not the intention of the revealing Spirit that all should be recorded in writing, however important the facts may appear. The evangelists did not record all the deeds and words of Jesus; the writer of the Acts did not deem it necessary for the work of the Apostles.

CHAPTER TWENTY-FIRST

PAUL'S THIRD APOSTOLIC TOUR

AFTER the tumult raised by the silversmiths at Ephesus had ceased, Paul called the disciples together, exhorted them to be steadfast in the faith, and took his leave. He departed earlier than he had anticipated and for a long time. At the end of his third tour he passed not far from Ephesus, but did not enter the city. He invited the clergy of Ephesus to the nearby town of Miletus, and delivered to them a wonderful speech, of which we give a synopsis in this chapter. On his way into Macedonia he broke his journey at Troas. He certainly stopped at Philippi, where he had announced the Gospel before, and whose citizens were so well disposed towards him. Frequently he had received alms from them. He tells us of all these particulars in his letter to the Philippians.

From Macedonia Paul went to Corinth to keep his promise and remained with the Corinthians three months during the winter. Alms had been collected in Achaia for the poor of Jerusalem, and Paul was about to take them to the beneficiaries, when the Jews laid in wait for him to rob him of his treasure (XX.3). He therefore changed his plans, and instead of sailing directly for Syria, and visiting Antioch on his way, he decided to go by the roundabout way of Macedonia. He was accompanied by Sopater of Berea, a kinsman of his (Rom. XXII.21). Aristarchus and Secundus of Thessalonica, Gaius of Derbe, Timothy, Tychicus and Trophimus of Asia. Tychicus, Paul's dearest brother and faithful minister, was as a rule the messenger bearing his orders to the various churches (Eph.VI.21). Trophimus was an Ephesian by birth and a convert from heathenism. On one occasion, Paul introduced him into the temple. The Jews considered that a desecration—a Gentile in the temple! Paul was seized on that account (Acts XXI.29). Trophimus was later on consecrated bishop by the Apostle and sent as a missionary to France, and became the first bishop of Arles. Luke joined the company at Troas.

The Acts tell us (XX.7) that on the first day of the week, that is, on Sunday, the faithful came together to break bread. The expression "to break bread" in the Primitive Church meant the celebration of the Holy Eucharist. We learn therefrom that the faithful met on Sunday for the celebration of the Holy Eucharist and Holy Communion, before that was enacted into law for the universal Church by Anacletus, the fourth successor of Peter. Paul protracted his discourse until midnight, when in the morning he would proceed on his journey.

In the beginning of the Church the Lord's Supper, as it was called, was celebrated in the evening, in imitation of Our Lord. We must admire the fervor

of Paul and the devotion of the audience in that
farewell speech protracted unto midnight. The
Lord's Supper followed upon the exhortation. We
learn from the very early writers that on Sundays
the faithful fasted until after Holy Communion, out
of respect, not because there was a precept to that
effect. There was a great number of lamps in the
upper chamber to light up the room and for decora-
tive purposes in the celebration of the Holy Eucharist. The room must have been crowded, because
we are informed that a young man had taken his
seat on the window sill. He was overpowered with
a deep sleep and fell down from the third loft to the
ground (XX.9). Eutychius, as he was named, was
taken up dead. What part the common enemy took
in the accident we do not know, but the sad event
cast a gloom upon the joyful meeting. Paul went
down immediately and laid himself upon the corpse,
not to find out whether he was really dead, there
was no doubt about it, but to recall him to life by
that symbolical act, as some prophets of the Old Testament had done before him. So did Elias raise to
life the widow's son (3 Kings XVII.21) and Eliseus
the dead child (4 Kings IV.34). Paul embraced him
and told the assembly: Be not troubled for his soul
is in him. Here is no question of an apparent death;
Paul did not say: His soul is still in him; but the
miracle accompanied the words, just as when Christ
said to the ruler: "Go thy way, thy son liveth"
(Jno. IV.50). Christ had foretold to His disciples
that they would do greater signs than He had done.

Ancient writers tell us that Eutychius afterwards followed St. John and died a martyr in Spain. We can imagine the joy of the community on account of this direct intervention of the omnipotent God. The risen young man went with the others into the upper chamber, and joined in the celebration of the Lord's Supper, which the Apostle apparently celebrated after the miracle. After that he partook of a fraternal meal with them and kept on exhorting them until daybreak, when he departed.

He had sent his companions by water to Asson on the east coast of Mysia with instructions to await his arrival. He made the trip by land, which made the distance from Troas much shorter and enabled him to tarry longer with the faithful at that place. At Asson they took Paul on board, and set sail for Mitylene, passed Chios and anchored at Samos, an island in the Ionian Sea. On the following day they landed at Miletus. Paul had determined not to touch Ephesus on this trip, lest he be prevented from reaching Jerusalem in time for the feast of Pentecost. While at Miletus he called the ancients of the church at Ephesus to him. The two towns were about forty miles apart. He wished to address the pastors of souls in a familiar way and to open his heart to them. He spoke to them as a loving father, who is aware of his approaching end, and gave to them the reasons for faithfulness in their pastoral duties. Paul's discourse will remain an enduring monument of the qualities demanded in the work of a minister of the Gospel. A short synopsis of it follows; the numbers indicate the verses in Chapter XX of the Acts.

Evangelical labor must be undertaken with a pure intention, directing it to the right purpose, which is, in the first place, the glory of God, Paul served God, not man (19); secondly, the salvation of souls, that men may do penance and embrace the faith of Christ (21) and so obtain the inheritance of the saints (32).

Such labor must be constant, continuous, without loss of time, as Paul's was from the first day and for all the time (18) night and day (31).

Labor must be protracted according to the requirements and the need of places (31). Paul worked among them for three years, a long time indeed for one who had to preach the Gospel over the whole Roman Empire.

Labor must be universal, both for persons—Jews and Gentiles—(31) and for places, publicly and from house to house (20).

Evangelical labor must be humble (19) fearless (24) patient in tribulations (19) generous and heroic even unto death (24) prudent with the weak (35) free from filthy lucre (33).

If circumstances make it necessary, the evangelical worker must be prepared to live from the work of his hands in conjunction with his ministry of the word (34).

To stimulate himself continually for that work, Paul was ever mindful of its excellence, because in its origin it is the ministry of the word, which he had received from the Lord Jesus (24); in its purpose it was to lead souls to the kingdom of God, by procuring for them the grace of God; in its exercise the duties are most serious.   Paul claimed that he was free from the blood of all, as he had never been guilty of spiritual homicide by causing a soul to be lost on his account.

In his discourse Paul addressed those whom the Holy Ghost had placed bishops to rule the Church of God.   We have explained above the difference between Bishops and Priests in the Primitive Church. He warns them that they must provide for their own salvation, so as to procure more efficaciously the salvation of the whole flock, entrusted to their care. He foretold them that after his departure ravening wolves would enter, and not spare the flock.   Such enemies would arise even from their own ranks; events soon proved the correctness of the prophecy. Hymeneus, Alexander, Phygellus and Hermogenes proved to be such wolves.

Paul claimed for himself the honor of having faithfully discharged the evangelical office, and could invite his hearers to be his followers as he was the follower of Christ (1 Cor. XI.1).

Paul had told them that they would see his face no more.   Great was the mutual love of Paul and his followers.   The people he was addressing were of the same sentiments as those to whom he wrote: You received me as an angel of God, even as Christ Jesus . . . you would have plucked out your own eyes and would have given them to me (Gal. IV.14–15). No wonder that the final parting on earth was so touching!   Luke tells us that all fell on their knees to find in prayer the strength to overcome their emotions; all wept and embraced him, and accompanied him to the ship. As the Acts express it, he was parted from them; to leave people he loved so well meant for Paul a severe interior battle (XXI.1).

Paul with his companions then sailed in a straight course, without anchoring anywhere to Coos, Rhodes, and Patara. The ship that had brought them so far was either bound for Patara, or followed the shores of Lysia, Pamphylia and Cilicia to Antioch. Paul found at Patara another ship ready to leave for Tyre. He took this ship so as to be in Jerusalem earlier, and therefore he gave up his desire to revisit Antioch. They left the island of Cyprus to the left, and came to Tyre where the ship would unload. The Gospel had been preached here before, but in proportion to the population the disciples were few, and they had to search for them. The missionaries remained here seven days. After that the whole community, the men with their wives and children, accompanied them beyond the city's gate, and before bidding each other goodbye, they all knelt down on the seashore and prayed. The inspired writer wished us to realize how Paul during his short stay had endeared himself to the Christians. They warned Paul not to go to Jerusalem; they felt that evil would befall him there, but it was not the Holy Ghost who dissuaded him, on the contrary an interior inspiration invited him to go.

From Tyre they sailed to Ptolemais, where they saluted the brethren; thence they proceeded to Cæsarea, where Philip the Deacon lived, whose work at Samaria we have had occasion to admire.   Philip had four daughters, all virgins and prophetesses. Luke mentions the latter fact, because they probably foretold Paul what dangers awaited him.   All four were honored as saints from the first centuries of Christianity.   Meanwhile another prophet, Agabus, the same who had foretold the general famine in the empire under Claudius, came in from Judea to Cæsarea. He came to the house of Philip, took Paul's girdle, bound his own hands and feet, and then solemnly said; "Thus saith the Holy Ghost: The man whose girdle this is, the Jews shall bind in this manner in Jerusalem, and shall deliver him into the hands of the Gentiles" (XXI.11).   Paul's companions and the Christians of Cæsarea used their best efforts to induce him to give up his trip.   Paul consoled them and protested that he was prepared not only to be bound but to die in Jerusalem.   All their pleadings availed not; they ceased their opposition, and all joined in saying: The will of the Lord be done!

CHAPTER TWENTY-SECOND

AFTER a painful farewell to his followers at Cæsarea, of whom many joined the pilgrims, Paul and his companions proceeded to Jerusalem. All knew that the faithful there through persecutions and robbery on the part of the Jews, had lost their property and were in great distress. Paul came to help them with the alms he had collected. Foreseeing that it would be next to impossible to find lodgings in a city crowded with visitors for the feast, they brought with them one Mnason, a Cyprian, who probably owned houses in Jerusalem, and with whom they would stay. No particulars are known about this man other than that he was an old disciple. Commentators tell us that Paul arrived about Pentecost in the year 58, the 14th year of Peter in Rome, the 2nd of Nero, the year in which the Blessed Mother of Jesus left the earthly Jerusalem for the heavenly Sion. In deference to St. James, the head of the Church in Jerusalem, Paul presented the pilgrims to him, and also to the seniors, and to the priests. About five years later in the seventh year of Nero, James after a most holy life was precipitated from the temple and finished with a potter's stick. There was at that time no other Apostle in Jerusalem. After a cordial exchange of greetings, Paul gave a detailed account of the great things God had done among the Gentiles by his ministry. They were all Christians and they naturally glorified God upon that report, but still they had their own views about Moses and the law. They began telling Paul of the thousands of Jewish converts, all zealous for the law, as he could see for himself. Addressing Paul they told him that they had heard that he taught the Jews who lived among the Gentiles to depart from Moses, not to circumcise their children, and not to walk according to the old customs. The accusation was completely false. Paul indeed taught that the ceremonial part of the law was abrogated, and that no one was obliged to submit to it, but he did not contend that the keeping of it was bad or illicit, nor did he prevent the Jews from submitting to it.

In regard to the prescriptions of the law we must mark three periods: Before the death of Christ, they were binding; after the death of Christ and up to a sufficient promulgation of the gospel, they were abrogated but the observance was not sinful; after that, observance of the law and of its prescriptions became sinful.

Paul was warned that the Jews hearing of his arrival would certainly come together, complain of and accuse him, and perhaps illtreat and fine him, unless he gave proofs of his zeal for the law. The faithful requested him to follow their advice as a way out of the difficulty. They had four men with the vow of the nazareate, which consisted in shaving the head, a legal ablution, and the offer of a sacrifice according to the law. He was to sanctify himself with them, and make an offering to defray the expenses of the four, who were probably too poor for a headshave and other incidentals, so that he be considered as a patron of Judaism and of the Jews. Paul, who desired to be all to all that he might gain all, followed the advice of St. James and of the faithful. After having gone through that ceremony of purification with the four men, he entered the temple and notified the congregation of what he had done. The Jews of Asia who had caused him so much trouble in the past, on seeing him in the temple, stirred up all the people, and laid their hands upon him. They claimed that he had offended the people, broken the law, and desecrated the temple by introducing Gentiles into that holy place. They knew that Trophimus of Ephesus was with him and they thought that he had introduced him in the temple, that is, in the atrium, for in the temple none but priests could enter, and in the holy of holies only the pontiff, and that only once a year. The whole city was in an uproar; the people rushed to the temple, drew Paul out, and immediately shut the doors. While they prepared to kill him, the Roman tribune of a band of soldiers in the Antonia fortress close to the temple, was informed of the general confusion. He at once, accompanied by soldiers and centurions, ran down to them. As soon as the Jews noticed their arrival upon the scene, they left off beating Paul. The tribune Claudius took charge of him and ordered him bound with two chains. He then questioned the uproarmakers who he was and what he had done. In the confusion all screamed different things so that he could not get any satisfactory answers to his questions. He took Paul to the military barracks. On the short distance between the two places the violence of the mob was such, that Paul had to be carried into the barracks by the soldiers. The multitude followed and cried out, as they had done a few years before in the case of his Master: Away with him! As he was about to be led into the castle, he requested the tribune to be allowed to speak. The tribune asked him: "Canst thou speak Greek? As Paul was speaking Greek, the tribune possibly suspected that he might be the Egyptian, who lately had raised a tumult and had led forth into the desert four thousand men that were murderers. This Egyptian had given himself out for the Messiah and had a great following of robbers, whose ranks were steadily increased and renewed, and who did much harm to the Jews, especially later at the siege of Jerusalem. Perhaps the question of the tribune to Paul implied that he could not be that man. Paul answered: I am a Jew of Tarsus in Cilicia, a citizen of no mean city. He then asked the tribune for permission to address the crowd. The tribune consented. Standing on the stairs, Paul beckoned with his hand and all were silent. Paul then began in Hebrew, that is, in Aramaic or Syro-Chaldean, called Hebrew, because it was the vernacular of the Jews.

He gave an account of his criminal life before his conversion, of his conversion, and of the special mission he had received from Jesus Christ. All went well until he told his audience that Christ had sent him to the Gentiles afar off (XXII.21). Then pandemonium broke out again, and they screamed: Away with such an one from the earth, for it is not fit that he should live! They kept up howling, threw off their garments, and cast dust into the air. They did so to show their disgust for the words of Paul, and to force a sentence of condemnation from the tribune, because he was a troublemaker for heaven and earth. How they longed to stone him to death! As the Apostle spoke in Hebrew, the tribune had probably not understood him, and suspected him guilty of an awful crime. To find it out he ordered him scourged and tortured. In doing so he went against the Roman criminal code, which forbade an inquiry to begin with punishment. After they had bound him with thongs Paul asked a centurion nearby: Is it lawful for you to scourge a man that is a Roman and uncondemned? (XXII.26.) He appealed to his citizenship. The tribune was immediately informed of the fact; he claimed that he had bought the freedom of Rome with a great sum, but Paul could go one better and protested that he was born so. The consequences of his act dawned upon the tribune; for treating a Roman citizen in that way, he had exposed himself to the wrath of the Romans.

The following day Paul was brought before the priests and the council, who had met by order of the tribune.   He began to speak, but it was only a minute before he was interrupted.   The high-priest ordered the bystanders to strike him on the mouth.   Paul's answer to the insult was: God shall strike thee, thou whited wall.   Your office demands that you judge according to the law, and here you order me to be struck against the law.   This supposed curse on the high-priest drew forth further abuse.   Paul claimed ignorance of the fact that at that time there was a high-priest.   His words were more in the form of a prophecy than of a curse.   The hypocrite was indeed struck, when in the year 66 he was killed, in the beginning of the Jewish war.   In those turbulent times the office of high-priest was often vacant; furthermore there was nothing to indicate that Ananias was the high-priest; Paul's ignorance was quite legitimate.

Paul did not lose his presence of mind and came forth with a new argument in his own defence.   As we have had frequent occasion to remark, the Jews were divided into Pharisees and Sadducees; they disagreed radically in their dogmatic belief.   Paul claimed to be a Pharisee and the son of a Pharisee, firmly believing the resurrection of the dead.   This assertion aroused the ire of the Sadducees, and placated the others, who now took up his defence, and openly professed that they found no evil in this man, and that perhaps a spirit or an angel had spoken to him. A quarrel between the two factions ensued. For fear that Paul should be pulled in pieces between the contestants, the tribune ordered him to be brought into the castle.

The following night the Lord stood by him and said: "Be constant for as thou hast testified of me in Jerusalem, so must thou bear witness also in Rome" (XXIII.12). The promise filled Paul with joy. He would announce Jesus not only in Jerusalem, the center of religion at that time, and at Athens, the mother of philosophy, but in Rome, the capital of the world, the chief in political power and in polytheism!

Meanwhile some of the Jews had sworn that they would not eat or drink before they killed Paul; forty of them had formed the conspiracy. Plans were discussed and adopted; the chief priests and the seniors were to request the tribune to bring Paul out for further investigation, and on the way they would kill him. A nephew of Paul had overheard the conversation, and immediately informed his uncle of it. Paul called a centurion, and requested him to lead the young man to the tribune, because he had something to tell him. The tribune took him by the hand, drew him aside and had a private conversation with him; he then dismissed him and commanded him to be silent about the interview. The tribune in dealing with a Roman citizen was not prepared to take any chances. He called two centurions and commanded them to have ready to move by nine o'clock

that night 200 soldiers, 70 horsemen, and two spear-
men, and to proceed to Cæsarea.   They were also to
provide beasts for Paul to sit on, and bring him safe
to Felix the Governor.   They were bearers of a letter
from the tribune to Felix.   The whole guard moved
during the night to Antipatris.   At that distance
from the city there was less danger of an ambush,
and therefore the horsemen were dismissed and
returned to the castle.   The others proceeded with
Paul to Cæsarea.   On arrival the centurions handed
the letter to the governor and presented Paul before
him.   The governor enquired from what province
Paul came, and on learning that he was from Cilicia,
he assured him that he would have an opportunity
to explain when his accusers arrived, and that in the
meantime he would be detained in Herod's judgment
hall.   Such a hall, also called pretorium, was the
official residence of a Roman governor in the provinces.   Herod the Great had formerly occupied, perhaps built, this palace.   Paul was not thrown into an
ordinary prison; the tone of Claudius Lysias' letter
was rather favorable to Paul.

CHAPTER TWENTY-THIRD

FIVE days after Paul's arrival in Cæsarea, a delegation composed of the high-priest Ananias, of some elders, and a lawyer and orator named Tertullus, came from Jerusalem to testify against Paul. Tertullus was well versed in Roman law, and an eloquent Latin scholar. The tribune Lysias, after having sent Paul on his way to Cæsarea, had informed the priests of what he had done, lest he should appear to deceive them. They then resolved at once to send the above delegation. Ananias was the most interested. As a Sadducee he hated Paul and Christ, and he had occasion to fear that he would be held responsible for the tumult in Jerusalem, and for his insult to the court, when he ordered Paul struck in the face. Tertullus is the spokesman before governor Felix, after Paul had been brought in.

The prosecutor began his speech with a base flattery to catch the benevolence of the governor. Felix is praised for the peace they enjoyed, and for all the improvements he had made, all of which the speaker gratefully acknowledged. The flattering terms were a tissue of lies. Tacitus in his history gives us the opposite impression. The gratitude of the Jews was such that shortly after the departure of Felix they lodged charges against him with the emperor; he was no longer the most excellent Felix then, although they had assured him that always and everywhere they had praised his benefits.

After the introduction Tertullus charged Paul with being a pestilent man, the author of all the trouble in the world, and especially of the late sedition in Jerusalem, and the profanator of the temple. The Jews corroborated the statements of their speaker. Paul's experiences in the various cities he had evangelized show the absurdity of the accusation; in nearly all the Jews had raised a sedition against him.

The defendant was given a sign by the governor to give his version and reply to the accusations. Trusting in his cause Paul dispensed with a stipulation of, the law allowing him a lawyer to plead for him. Felix had been governor of various provinces of the empire; he had been appointed to the governorship of Judea two years previously by Claudius shortly before the latter's death. Paul trusted in the governor's integrity; he pleaded his innocence and denied all the charges against him, none of which, he claimed, his accusers would prove. He fearlessly upheld what they called heresy or the sect of the Nazarene, his firm belief in the written word of God, the resurrection of the dead and his intention to persevere without offence to God or man. He informed the governor that only twelve days before he had come to Jerusalem to adore, and to bring relief to the poor and the needy; he added that he had not profaned the temple.   Paul threw the blame for the sedition on some Jews from Asia, who had inflicted almost deadly wounds on him and who should be here to prosecute the case.   The Apostle closed his defence with the ironical remark that the only accusation against him can be no other than his public assertion concerning the resurrection of the dead.

The governor deferred sentence until the tribune Lysias could be heard, and claimed to have more certain knowledge of the Christian religion than he could gather from the hearing.   From his stay in Judea and his governorship of adjoining provinces, and also from the report of the many Christians of Cæsarea, where the new religion had been introduced by Roman soldiers (X), he knew better and refused to condemn, because he was convinced of Paul's innocence; at the same time he was afraid to release him, lest he should offend the Jews.   He sheltered himself behind the information that Lysias should give, and ordered a centurion to keep Paul, but to treat him gently and to allow any of his friends to minister unto him.

After a few days Felix came into the courtroom accompanied by his wife Drusilla.   It is not certain why the sacred writer added these details.   Perhaps to call attention to the fact that she was anything but a respectable woman; she had been the wife of two others, and Felix had enticed her away from the last, as contemporary pagan writers tell us.   Having been a Jewess she was curious enough to induce her adulterous husband to question Paul about the difference between Christianity and Judaism. Paul's explanation did not effect their conversion; the known truth made them all the greater criminals. Paul thundered against adultery, as John the Baptist had done before him. Drusilla was a daughter of Herod Agrippa, who killed James and imprisoned Peter.

Felix was terrified but not converted; he allowed Paul to move about in the city. Money was even at that time an inducement to unscrupulous rulers. Felix had learned from Paul himself that he had brought money to Jerusalem, and he felt confident that his admirers would purchase his liberty. Paul despised this base venality, and rather than yield preferred to stay in prison and to be sent eventually to Nero.

Two years had passed since the appointment of Felix; his term had expired; he was succeeded by Portius Festus. Felix had left Paul in jail to please the Jews. Shortly after taking charge of his office Festus paid a visit to Jerusalem. The chief priests and the principal Jews hastened to meet him, and to request one particular favor of him. The request consisted in this that Paul should be brought back to Jerusalem; they had the intention to lay in wait to kill him on the way. Festus did not grant the request; he understood their malevolence, possibly he had heard of the conspiracy, and told them that Paul would be detained at Cæsarea, which was the judgment seat. He suggested that as he would very shortly return to Cæsarea, those able to go might accompany him, and accuse Paul if he was guilty; some did accept the invitation.

After a stay of eight or ten days Festus started on his return trip, and the day after his arrival he sat in the judgment seat and commanded Paul to be brought before him. The Jews made many and grievous accusations, but they could not prove them. Paul told the court that he had not offended in any way against the law of the Jews, nor against the temple, nor against Cæsar. Festus in order to please the Jews, asked him whether he was prepared to go to Jerusalem and there be judged by him. Paul refused; he stood before Cæsar's court and expected to be judged by it. He intimated that he was prepared to die, if he had injured the Jews, or done anything worthy of death, but if no such accusation was proved against him, he refused to be delivered to them. Paul was a Roman citizen and had a right to be tried by a Roman court; he could not even be tried against his will by the provincial Roman authorities. He did not wish to spend more time in prison than necessary and thus to be prevented from exercising his apostolic ministry; he desired an end to it whatever it might be. For that reason he appealed to Cæsar. We know already that he wished to go to Rome (XIX.21) and that the Lord had expressly promised the granting of that desire.

Paul appealed, not for his own life, but for the welfare of the Church; he appealed to the very man whom he is accused of having offended, because he had more than sufficient experience to show that he was nowhere safe in Judea or anywhere else from the snares of the Jews. He hoped perhaps to conciliate the sympathy of Nero for himself and for the Christians, or at least to die a martyr's death in the capital of the world. Festus conferred with his council whether Paul's appeal should be sustained or rejected; if he was the author of the sedition attributed to him, he could not be sent to Rome but had to be punished on the spot. The councillors found that he was not, and that therefore the appeal should stand. The governor's decision was: To Cæsar you have appealed, to Cæsar you shall go.

Some days later king Agrippa and Bernice came down to Cæsarea to offer their congratulations to Festus on his appointment to the governorship. This Agrippa was the brother of Drusilla and of Bernice. As Luke here connects the two names of Agrippa and Bernice, we may infer that they were living in incest. It is hard to say who of the four Herods, of whom the Bible makes mention, is the worst. Herod the Ascalonite was the murderer of the Innocents, and would have been of Christ, if he had found Him. His son mocked Christ and beheaded John the Baptist. His grandson imprisoned Peter and killed James. The great-grandson now desired to judge Paul.

Festus told his visitors the history of Paul; Agrippa expressed a desire to hear the man; the request was granted, he would see him the following day. Agrippa and Bernice arrived in great pomp into the courtroom. They must have forgotten that about 18 years before their father was struck in that very city by an angel and eaten up by worms (XII.23). They were surrounded by tribunes and

by the principal men of the city. On the order of
Festus, Paul was brought in. The governor introduced Paul as the man, whom the whole multitude
accused and considered unworthy to live, but in
whom he found nothing worthy of death; he had appealed to Cæsar and Festus had decided to send
him. Yet he was troubled about the appeal, because
there was no case or at least no conviction, and he
was at a loss to know how he would word his letter
to Cæsar without giving positive facts. He therefore brought him before the gathering and especially
before king Agrippa in order that a fresh examination might bring out facts for him to write about.
Festus realized the foolishness of his position in send-
ing a man to be judged by the highest tribunal without even specifying what the corpus delicti was.

Agrippa invited Paul to speak in his own defence.
This furnished him the unexpected opportunity to
give an account of his life, conversion, and calling.
Christ had foretold to Paul that he would preach His
name before kings (IX.15); here was the first chance
and he eagerly seized it; he addressed Agrippa, who
for his accurate knowledge of the law is even praised
in the Talmud. Without flattery or lie he captivated
the benevolence of the king. His eloquent account
of his early life as a pharisee and as a persecutor of
the Church, of his conversion and of his work as an
Apostle, made a deep impression on some, but it left
Festus indifferent. Festus interrupted Paul and cried
out in a loud voice: Paul, thou art beside thyself;
much learning doth make thee mad (XXVI.24).

Festus was a heathen; Paul's exposition of Christ's passion and resurrection, his vision, his ardor in speaking of mysteries, which he could not understand, appeared to him as so many expressions of a diseased brain. Paul is treated as his Master was before him. He denied the charge and claimed that his were words of truth and soberness; he appealed for confirmation of all he had said to the king; the facts in his case could not be hidden from him, for they were not done in a corner but in clear daylight to the knowledge of all. Paul then abruptly asked the king whether he believed the prophets; he anticipated his answer and said: I know that thou believest (27). Paul argued that if he believed the prophets, he had to believe in Christ. Agrippa answered: In a little thou persuadest me to be a Christian (28). Paul's argument had made some impression on the king; the Apostle expressed the hope that all who heard him might be entirely convinced, as he himself was, but the teaching of the gospel did not sufficiently appeal to an incestuous king in the midst of all that pomp. Notwithstanding that, Paul wished his conversion without desiring for him or any one else to be treated as he was; Paul was chained while delivering his speech. Agrippa, the governor, Bernice, and the councillors rose and discussed the case among themselves. They all agreed that Paul had done nothing worthy of death or of bands. Agrippa expressed the verdict of all to Festus: This man might have been set at liberty, if he had not appealed to Cæsar (32). Agrippa's conclusion was indeed a lame one. Paul should have been freed and the appeal would have fallen, but the king did not wish to offend the Jews by freeing him; to please them he ordered that Paul be sent as a prisoner to Cæsar.

CHAPTER TWENTY-FOURTH

PAUL ON HIS WAY TO ROME

FESTUS the governor of Syria followed the judgment of Agrippa and Paul was to be sent to Rome. He was placed in the custody of the centurion Julius, who would be his guard on the long journey. Paul had two of his disciples as companions—Luke the writer of the Acts, and Aristarchus, a Macedonian convert. In those days there was no regular passenger service between Italy and Asia Minor; they had to wait for a merchantman. A coasting ship from Adrumetum had arrived at Cæsarea, and Paul with his companions was put on board of it. The voyage was begun in the fall of 60. The next day they anchored at Sidon; Julius treated Paul very courteously and allowed him to land to see his friends and take care of himself. After unloading and loading they set sail in a northerly direction along the coast of Cyprus leaving the island to the left, because the winds were contrary. They came to Lystra the home of Timothy. The centurion here found a ship bound for Italy, and removed his prisoners into it. Owing to head winds they made very little progress for several days; they came to a promontory then known as Gnidus, the extremity of Asia Minor, and moved in the direction of Crete. Coasting along the island they came to a place called Good-havens, in the south of Crete. Much time had elapsed since they weighed anchor at Cæsarea, and navigation now was dangerous. The great fast of the Jews was passed, which shows that it was then towards the end of September 60, after the autumnal equinox. With the ancients navigation then came to an end and was not resumed until the middle of March.

Paul after a long experience knew something of the dangers of the sea (2 Cor. XI.26). Speaking rather by divine inspiration than from observation, he warned his fellow travelers of the dangers ahead, not only for lading and ship but for their own safety. In a question so important for a prisoner to be allowed to give his advice showed that Paul had gained the greatest confidence of his companions. The pilot, however, and the owner of the ship were of a different opinion and it carried more weight with the centurion than Paul's. The majority thought best to reach Phenice, if possible, and winter there; in this port they would be protected against the prevailing western winds. With a light southern breeze blowing they proceeded and kept close to the island. Soon after they encountered a typhoon, a strong north-easterly wind that drove them out to sea. From the description given by the inspired writer (XXVII) who was in it, it must have been a fearful storm that drove them off the small island of Cauda. They tried to manipulate the ship as well as they could; they cast overboard whatever seemed a hindrance; there was now fear of being driven on a sandbank. No sun or star had been seen for several days; they had no compass to guide them, all hope of saving their lives was abandoned, says St. Luke. In such weather no food could be prepared and all had to submit to a prolonged fast. In those dreadful circumstances, Paul stood in the midst of them and told them that if they had followed his advice they would have prevented all this harm and loss, but he invited them all to be of good cheer. He foretold them the destruction of the ship, but also the safety of each one of them. He explained a vision he had during the preceding night: "An angel of the God to whom I belong and whom I serve stood by me and said to me: 'Fear not, Paul, thou must be brought before Cæsar; and behold God hath given thee all them that sail with thee'" (XXVII.24). He repeated that they should be of good cheer and that they would come to a certain island.

The fourteenth night had now come; they were sailing in the Adria sea, not in the Adriatic between Italy and Dalmatia, but that part of the Mediterranean between Italy, Greece and Africa, which the ancients so called; it was about midnight. The shipmen suspected that they were near land; their delicate ears had perhaps heard the noise of the raging waves beating the coast. To make sure they sounded and found 20 fathoms; a little while later they found only 15. With this sudden rise they had reason to fear that the violence of the storm would soon throw the ship on the rocks and cause it to be broken up, and that in the middle of the night.   To prevent this they cast out four anchors from the stern.   The shipmen did not trust to the anchors with the ship under the wind and so near shore.   They were preparing to let down the life boat under pretext to cast out some more anchors from the bow, when Paul said to the centurion and to the soldiers (there were 276 men on board): Except these stay in the ship you cannot be saved (31).   Paul told this to the centurion and to the soldiers, not to the pilot or to the master, because these were in league with the other shipmen.   God indeed had promised that no one would perish, but under the tacit condition that all human means should be exhausted.   The soldiers appreciated Paul's warning.   They cut off the ropes of the boat, and let it fall down and drift away.   At dawn Paul besought them all to take some food; they had been fasting for two weeks and needed new strength for the struggle that was to follow; he promised them again that not a hair would fall from their head and that all would be saved.   Paul set the example, and first saying grace he began to eat bread.   Feeling now reassured they all followed his example.   After the meal they cast the wheat into the sea in order to lighten the boat; the cargo was thrown overboard before this, now the provisions went, which for 276 men must have made quite a weight.

It took some time to take a meal and lighten the ship, but then the shipmen could examine the coast at their leisure; it was now day.   They did not know the land, but they noticed the mouth of a creek, now called St. Paul's Bay, on the north-east coast of Malta. They thought of running the ship up its sandy shores; they raised the anchors, loosened the rudderbands, hoisted the topsail on the foremast, so as to force the big ship farther ashore. The forepart stuck fast and remained immovable, but the stern was exposed to the violence of wind and sea, and was fast being broken up.

Another difficulty now presented itself. What was to be done with the prisoners? because they might swim ashore and escape. The soldiers' counsel was that they should be killed; the centurion prevented this, Paul one of his prisoners ranked too high in his estimation. He ordered therefore that those who could swim should swim ashore first; of the others some were carried ashore on boards, others saved themselves with other parts of the wreckage.

The inspired history of this voyage and of the shipwreck of St. Paul is most interesting in its minute details, many of which are borne out by contemporary writers. In his second letter to the Corinthians Paul writes that he was shipwrecked three times, but as the letter was written before this occurrence, Paul was in reality wrecked four times.

All soon found out that they were safely landed on the island of Malta. Providence had directed this course of events for the good of the Maltese. Paul and his co-workers converted them and gave them Publius for their first bishop. A constant tradition there enables us to admit that Paul baptized all his ship companions. The faith was implanted so strongly on the island that it did not fail even under the domination of the Moors. The Barbarians showed great courtesy towards the shipwrecked. The sacred writer calls the inhabitants of Malta Barbarians, because they did not speak Greek or Latin, and were of African origin. At that time they were under the dominion of Rome and belonged to the province of Sicily. The hospitable barbarians kindled a wood fire, and led the 276 shipwrecked into a huge building, where they could dry their clothes and warm themselves. Paul again gave proof of his strenuous activity, humanity and humility by gathering a bundle of sticks himself. He had not noticed the presence of a viper in the bundle, the cold had benumbed it. When he put the sticks on the fire, the viper revived and fastened on his hand. The barbarians saw this, and as they knew that Paul was a prisoner, they concluded among themselves that he was a murderer, and that divine vengeance did not suffer him to live; they looked upon the bite of a viper as sure death. Paul meanwhile shook off the beast into the fire, and no harm was done to him (XXVIII). The onlookers expected that the bitten hand would swell, and Paul would fall down suddenly and die. Seeing that he was not hurt they changed their minds and concluded that he was a god.

Publius, the chief man of the island, owned extensive property in that section. He entertained Paul, Luke, Aristarchus and perhaps the centurion very courteously for three days. Publius' father lay sick of a fever, and of a bloody flux. Paul came in to the sick man, prayed, laid his hands on him, and miraculously cured him. The report of this miracle soon spread over the whole island, and all who were afflicted with disease came to Paul and were cured. A grateful people bestowed great honors on Paul and his companions, and provided all that was necessary for the voyage.

After a three months' stay on Malta, probably in the beginning of February 61, more than a month before navigation generally opened with the ancients, they found a ship from Alexandria that had wintered in the island, ready to set sail for Italy. Its sign was that of the Castors—Castor and Pollux—who were the usual protectors of the shipmen. The sailors in olden times placed their ships under the protection of the gods, whose image the Phœnicians engraved at the bow, and the Alexandrians painted or engraved on both sides of the stern.

They set sail for Syracuse, where they remained for three days. Sicily had received the faith from St. Peter as also its first bishops. Ancient writers tell us that the bishop of Syracuse received Paul with unspeakable joy; Paul in his bands was looked upon as a glorious champion of the faith. For three days he was the guest of bishop Marcianus, and undoubtedly did for the cause of Christ all he could.

Compassing by the shore, the ship again made for the land, in a small inlet between Taormina and Messina, about ten miles from the latter city. An ancient tradition places the landing of St. Paul near the spot where later St. Placid built his monastery, on a hill overlooking the bay. A contrary wind was probably the cause of this diversion. In sight of Messina they then crossed over to the mainland— to Reggio in Calabria. Luke is silent on many points of interest; he does not mention the conversion of the people of Reggio on Paul's visit, short as it was, only one day. Old documents of the same century, written in Greek and afterwards translated into Latin, and preserved in the diocesan archives of Reggio attest that Paul instructed and baptized many, and left them Stephen as first bishop. Stephen was one of Paul's companions on this trip and hailed from Nicea. He continued the work begun by Paul, and in one of the early persecutions died a martyr after a glorious profession of faith, together with the three saintly women Agnes, Felicitas, and Perpetua. Many other illustrations are given in these documents of Paul's miracles and zeal.

From Reggio assisted by a most favorable wind they covered the great distance to the bay of Naples in one day. The bay was then called the Bay of Pozzuoli. This was the port for ships from the Orient to Italy, especially for freighters bringing in wheat from Alexandria, as Seneca and Suetonius attest. The Jewish historian, Josephus, tells us that the busy port of Pozzuoli had attracted many Jews. No wonder that Paul went at once in search of the brethren, that is, the Jews converted to Christ. Tradition has it that Pozzuoli was visited by another Apostle—St. Peter—about the year 42 or 44 on his way from the east to Rome and that he had celebrated the holy mysteries there. At the request of the faithful Paul was allowed to tarry with them for seven days; he must have gained great confidence with the centurion to obtain that permission. The sacred writer does not give us any details of Paul's work in Pozzuoli; the tireless worker did here what he had done everywhere else.

The last stretch of the journey now began; it was to be made by land. There were two roads from Pozzuoli to Rome; one via Capua and thence by the Appian Way, the other followed the coast to Gaeta and then at Terracina joined the first. The Acts do not inform us by what road Paul went, but an old Greek manuscript edited by Tischendorf informs us that he went to Baja and thence to Terracina. The direction of the Appian Way near Rome is well known; from the Capena gate between the Celius and the Aventine it goes towards the Alban mountains and then enters the Pontine marches. On this road we find the two stations mentioned in the Acts—the forum Appii and the Three Taverns. The first was about 43 miles from Rome on the Appian way and the other 23. The road at the time of St. Paul was in a horrible condition on account of the very frequent inundations; it remained in bad shape until Trajan raised the level. Both Strabo and Horace have left us an unfavorable description of it. Paul may have been compelled to go part of the way by boat, as the poet had done before him.

During the seven days Paul spent at Pozzuoli, a

messenger could easily reach Rome to apprise the faithful of his early arrival. Many of them went out to meet him as far as the places we have mentioned. They were most anxious to see the great Apostle, from whom they had received such an interesting letter about three years before, but they never expected to meet him in the condition of a prisoner bound in chains. The sight impressed St. Paul; he thanked God and took courage. Another Apostle had converted the Romans, whom Paul saw before him; their devotion and noble sentiments excited in him a great desire to have a share in the conversion of the others. Peter had come to Rome in the reign of Claudius, but he was not there in 61 when Paul arrived, nor was he there in 58, when Paul wrote his letter to the Romans. In the first year of Nero, the Jews who had been expelled by Claudius began to return to the capital. Recent discoveries of Jewish cemeteries prove that the Jews were numerous in Rome in its imperial days.

The Acts tell us that Paul was permitted to dwell by himself, but under a military guard. The centurion must have handed him over to the governor of the military camp and we may suppose that Paul had his lodgings nearby. This fortified camp had been built by Tiberius for an imperial bodyguard of 10,000 men. The present military barracks have replaced the old camp of the Pretorian guards, who were disbanded by Constantine. The camp was a little beyond the present railway terminal station.

The favorable reports of Festus and of the centurion Julius had secured for Paul his partial liberty; and he had many friends even in Nero's palace, as their greetings to the Philippians show (IV.22). He stopped for a while with a friend, perhaps with Aquila his host at Corinth, who had preceded him to Rome (Rom. XVI.3) but always under military guard, which means in the language of those days that Paul's left arm was chained to the right arm of a soldier. The first three days after his arrival were devoted to the Christians, who had received him so lovingly and whom he longed to see (Rom. I.11). He found that all things appertaining to religion had been wisely arranged by Peter, and therefore he consecrated, as usual, his first labors to the Jews. He thought it prudent to approach them first, because they might be interested in the suit pending against him. As he was not allowed to go to their synagogue, he invited the chief of the Jews to his own hired lodging. He desired to address them in order to remove their possible prejudiced opinions, that might prove obstacles to their conversion, and to explain his own unenviable position. He denied any guilt against the Jewish race, and added that he was forced to appeal and professed his affection for them. Paul suspected that he had been accused and calumniated with them, but he was mistaken. The Jews claimed that they never had heard anything disparaging of him, either by letter or from a visitor. They expressed a desire to hear him, for they had learned that this sect—the Christian Religion—was being contradicted everywhere. They agreed upon a day.

for a meeting, at which very many assisted and which lasted a whole day. Paul proved to them from Moses and the Prophets that Jesus was the Messiah. After a long debate some believed, but others did not. Before they departed without agreeing Paul made only one more remark, and it was that whereas they as a nation would not hear, the word of salvation had been sent to the Gentiles, who would hear. Upon this the Jews left and continued quarreling among themselves.

Paul remained for two years in his hired lodging, received all who came to him, preached with confidence and without restraint the kingdom of God, and taught all about the Lord Jesus Christ. We have had occasion to remark that Paul from prison wrote several of his letters, and continued his interest in the churches, which he had founded. Baronius, the great historian, thinks that as Paul's case concerned religious matters, Nero gave it over to the pagan priests, who in their hatred of the Jews dismissed it.

Luke here ends the inspired history of the Primitive Church in year 63, in the fifth year of Nero, after two years of Paul's imprisonment. From now on we must be guided by the writings of St. John, and the epistles of Peter and Paul, that are posterior to that date, and to history as related by uninspired human historians, and subjected to strict criticism.

CHAPTER TWENTY-FIFTH

PAUL had been freed by Nero, or as he explained it to his beloved disciple Timothy, he had been delivered out of the mouth of the lion. We have attributed his deliverance to the letter of Festus, governor of Judea, who had stated that neither he, nor his predecessor, nor the tribune, could find Paul guilty of any offence. Tacitus gives us another reason. A public demonstration had been offered Nero on the restoration of his health, and perhaps to cover over by a humane act the horrible deed of killing his own mother—Agrippina—an amnesty was granted on that occasion to Paul and his fellow prisoners.

History does not tell us in detail what happened between the recovery of his freedom and his return to Rome to be cast into prison again, previous to his execution. Paul evidently had not anticipated this turn of affairs, when he wrote his letter to the Romans. He had told them (XV.24) that he intended to go to Spain and that on the way he hoped to see them. We may suppose that after securing his freedom he carried out his original plan and went to Spain. The fact that the bishop and father of the faithful in Spain had been beheaded by Herod in

Jerusalem may have inspired the desire of preaching the Gospel there and of taking St. James' place with his orphaned children.   The oldest records tell us that in 64 Paul was in Spain.   On his way out he had Philemon, Timothy and other disciples as companions.   Sergius Paul, of whom we treated before when he was proconsul of Cyprus (Acts XIII.7) and who after his conversion had been made bishop of Narbonne, accompanied Paul to Spain.   Several disciples of Paul are ranked among the martyrs of the Primitive Church in Spain.   Ancient writers inform us that after his first imprisonment in Rome, Paul revisited his dear converts of Syria, Asia, Macedonia, and Greece, as he himself had expressed that wish in his letter to the Philippians and to Philemon.   After that he returned to Rome to assist Peter in his fight against Simon the Magician and against Nero.

Peter came to Rome for the first time about the year 42.   How often he left the city and returned the Acts do not say, but he returned there a last time shortly before his death under Nero.   Peter was absent when Paul arrived as a prisoner in 61.   Professor Marucchi, the renowned archeologist, from whom we borrow these details, admits that Peter was there in 64, at the time of the terrible persecution of Nero, because in his letter he makes allusion to Rome as Babylon.   The fearful conflagration, that destroyed a great part of the city in July 64, was the occasion of the persecution; Jews and Christians were at that time considered as one class, although all Christians had not been Jews.   Suspicion for causing the fire fell upon the Jews, who in turn threw the blame on the Christians and claimed that they had nothing in common with the new religion. Tacitus has left us a vivid description of Nero's ferociousness in burning alive the first martyrs in his gardens of the Vatican. He says: Nero added mockery to insult for those about to die. Covered with animal skins they were to be torn to pieces by wild dogs, or nailed to crosses, or burned alive to light up a dark night. St. Clement in his letter to the Corinthians writes of Christian heroines, exposed barbarously to ferocious tortures, such as described in pagan mythology. The persecution lasted up to 68 when Nero died; it was not limited to Rome but extended also to the provinces. Peter had survived the tempest of 64, as is certain from certain expressions in his letter.

There are various opinions concerning the year of the martyrdom of Peter and Paul; but most writers adhere to the year 67 for the following reasons. St. Jerome attests that Seneca died two years before the Apostles, and from Tacitus we learn that Nero's teacher ended his life during the consulate of Silius Nerva and Atticus Vestino, in 65.

There is no certainty in regard to the exact date. In the fourth century the feast of their martyrdom was kept on the 29 of June. Possibly this may have been the date of the translation of their relics to the Appian Way.

There are no contemporary and authentic acts concerning the martyrdom of the two Apostles. There are, however, most ancient traditions carefully recorded in the days of peace and that have come down to us. These traditions attest as an undeniable historical fact the coming of the two Apostles to Rome, their foundation of the Roman church, and their glorious martyrdom under Nero. It is certain that in the second century the faithful had a written version of the passion of Peter. The tradition concerning the manner of their death must be considered as authentic. Paul was a Roman citizen; an ignominious death in his case was not permissible. The Gospel of St. John makes clear allusion to the crucifixion of Peter, and as Origen attests, it was a well known fact that he was crucified head down.

The two Apostles did not suffer martyrdom on the same spot. Paul was beheaded about three miles from Rome near the Ardea Road, left of the way to Ostia. The place is now called Tre Fontane, or the Three Fountains, and owes its name to an ancient tradition that Paul's head after being severed from the body made three distinct leaps, the exact spots being marked by three fountains that welled forth.

Where we have a constant and uniform tradition in regard to the place of Paul's martyrdom, various learned opinions are held even now in regard to the spot where Peter was crucified. Some hold that the Vatican hill was the spot; others believe the Janiculus to be the place. The most ancient tradition favors the Vatican; it attests that he was martyred near Nero's palace before the obelisk. The description given indicates the stadium or the circus in the villa of Nero, generally called in the documents Nero's palace. The obelisk remained in its original place up to the time of Sixtus V (1585–1590), when it was removed to the grand piazza in front of St. Peter's Basilica, where it is to-day. In recent centuries an opinion has been expressed in favor of the Janiculus, on the very spot where we admire the round little church, planned by Bramante, but it does not rest upon any ancient documents.

The most authentic monuments of the Apostles are undoubtedly the two sepulchres of the Vatican and of the Appian Way. They were well known in the second century. Cajus, one of the great historical authorities of that day, wrote the following words as a refutation to some heretics: "I can show you the trophies of the Apostles, whether you go to the Vatican or to the Ostian Way, you will find the trophies of those who founded this Church." These tombs could not but be recognized by all for the inscriptions they bore. In the days of Constantine the historian Eusebius said that the fact of the death of the two Apostles is spendidly confirmed by their monuments in the Roman cemeteries. In the fourth century Optatus of Milevi quotes against the Donatists the memories of the Apostles, which in the language of that time means their tombs. Towards the end of the same century St. Jerome speaks of the tomb of St. Peter as of a monument venerated on the Vatican by the whole Christian world. Prudentius, the great Christian poet in the beginning of the fifth century, indicates with precision the place of the two tombs on the two opposite sides of the Tiber.   Besides these authentic and genuine evidences there are many more, such as the grand basilicas built by Constantine on the two sacred spots, the itineraries of the pilgrims, the sepulchral inscriptions, etc.

All these documents attest the universal conviction of the Christian world that the two tombs were precisely on the same spots where we venerate them today, on the Vatican and on the Ostian Way.

The two primitive tombs of the Apostles were, like all others, outside of the city, and formed little compartments in the property of a Christian; these were selected because of their proximity to the place of their death.   Of the original rooms nothing is left, as both were taken into the splendid basilicas built over them.

The many tomb inscriptions found in the excavations for the new basilica prove that the area, in which St. Peter's tomb was found, was a burial ground in the imperial days.   That area began to be used in 64 as a cemetery for the martyrs under Nero. It is quite natural that Peter himself should be buried there, as his successors were up to 202.   In that year the bishops of Rome selected for their official burial place the cemetery of Callixtus; that of the Vatican had become too small.   Discoveries of sarcophagi at the time of the excavations for the new basilica in the seventeenth century, and among them that of St. Linus, the immediate successor of St. Peter, which had for an inscription only the name Linus, prove that the first bishops of Rome were buried there.

The tomb with the precious relics had to be guarded against the invasion of the barbarians in the fifth century. It was thoroughly covered and hidden in 846, when the Saracens besieged Rome. After that date it has never been exposed again. In 1592 Pope Clement VIII accompanied by two Cardinals, one of whom was the famous Cardinal Bellarmini, had an opening made and saw the sarcophagus of Peter with the gold cross of Constantine on it; for fear of profanation he ordered the opening closed at once. It is to-day hidden under the grottoes of the present basilica.

The body of St. Paul was buried in a field owned by a pious Roman matron named Lucina, on the Ostian Way, a little more than a mile from the city's gate. Fr. Grisar, another learned archæologist, tells us that the first basilica was built over the spot by Constantine; Emperor Valentinian II replaced it in 386 by a larger one, which corresponds exactly with the lines of the present basilica, built after the fire of 1823.

These two imposing structures are enduring monuments of the death of the two Apostles in Rome. It is possible that their remains have been temporarily moved, but it is certain that Linus, the immediate successor of Peter and the others of the first century were buried near the body of Blessed Peter on the Vatican Hill.

After the peace of Constantine these tombs gradually became objects of greater veneration. Towards the end of the fourth century Damasus adorned them with metrical inscriptions. The translation of one of these is as follows: If you wish to know, Peter and Paul have been here. We confess that these Apostles came to us from the Orient, but having shed their blood for Jesus Christ they became Romans, and Rome merited to keep the bodies of its citizens.

It would be hard to indicate the various places of temporary residence of St. Peter while in Rome, nor does history register the vicissitudes of the episcopal chair of Peter, as now preserved in the greatest church of Christendom.

CHAPTER TWENTY-SIXTH

THE INSPIRED WRITERS OF THE NEW TESTAMENT

PROMINENT figures in the history of the Primitive Church were the inspired writers, who under the influence and inspiration of the Holy Ghost, left us a summary of the whole Christian faith and practice. In the four gospels they give us the life and the work of its author—Jesus Christ—the Saviour of the world; in the other parts they show the fulfilment of the mission intrusted by Christ to the Apostles, and the prophetic mission of the Church in the course of ages up to the end of time.

We add a brief notice of each author and a short review of his writings in the order that his name appears in the sacred volume beginning with the Gospels.

ST. MATTHEW

Matthew, also called Levi, was a Jew and a Galilean. He was receiver of public money, when Christ called him to the apostolate. He lived at Capharnaum near the sea of Tiberias. His office made him hateful to the Jews, with whom publican and sinner were synonymous. The reason of this hatred must be found in the fact that these officeholders were either Gentiles, or Jews who connived in a social and business manner with the Roman tyrants of Palestine. The Jews at that time had to pay to the Romans a head tax and a property tax; in addition to that they had to pay for a permit to the public pastures, tithes on their crops, and custom duties on imports and exports. The publicans, less contumacious and less proud than the pharisees were more likely candidates for conversion.

The Gospel according to St. Matthew is the first book of the New Testament and also the first in the order of its composition. It was originally written in Aramaic, then the vernacular of the Jews. St. Matthew wrote in Palestine most probably before the expulsion of the Apostles from the Holy City in the year 42 during the persecution of Herod Agrippa. He wrote for the Palestine converts from Judaism, especially for those who lived in and around Jerusalem.

His purpose was above all to show that Jesus is the promised Messiah, in an historico-apologetic way, greatly differing in that respect from the rather dogmatic method of St. John in his Gospel. Matthew gives us the active rather than the contemplative part in the life of Jesus, and more precepts for righteous living.

The argument or the subject matter concerns the origin and the hidden life of Christ, His public life, His preaching, and His miracles up to the time of His Ascension, which he does not mention.

ST. MARK

The name of Mark has frequently occurred in the preceding chapters. He was chiefly the interpreter of Peter, although he had also been a disciple of Paul, and under his two chiefs was a great missionary. Some have contended that in the Acts two persons of the same name are mentioned, but it is more probable that the same person is designated. There is no doubt as to the authorship of the second Gospel.

The most ancient writers tell us that Mark wrote in Rome, chiefly for the Romans what he had learned from the lips of Peter. This explains how in recording the preaching of Peter, many facts are omitted that would tend to the glory and the honor of the author's chief, showing on the one hand absence of flattery on the part of Mark, and on the other great humility on the part of Peter.

There is a great difference of opinion as to what precise time this gospel was written, ranging from the year 42 to the year 96, whether during the lifetime of Peter or not, is not known for certain. Mark as an introduction begins with the baptism of John the Baptist, the baptism of Christ and His retreat into the desert. Then he gives us the public ministry of Christ in Galilee, and in and around Jerusalem, and finally His Resurrection and Ascension. He insists with emphasis upon the formation of the Apostles.

ST. LUKE

Luke was a companion and co-laborer of Paul. In a letter of Paul (Col. IV.14) he is called a physician. Luke was not a Jew by birth; he was an Antiochian, who probably learned the Christian religion from and was baptized by Paul or Barnabas. Some have thought that Luke was one of the 72 disciples and that he was one of the two disciples of Emmaus, but this is not likely. He says himself that he received from the Apostles what he conveys in his Gospel; he did not see Christ. Luke was among the four evangelists the best versed in the Greek language; he wrote rather for Greeks than for Hebrews; being a physician he must have had the advantages of a more classical education. Some writers include in his education Syrian and Aramaic, grammar, poetry, and rhetoric. Luke merited the praises of St. Paul (2 Cor. VIII.18).

Luke is reported to have been a renowned painter; the oldest painting of the Mother of God is ascribed to him.

There is no absolute certainty as to where and how Luke died, and where he wrote his Gospel; he wrote it in the year 63. It was addressed to one Theophilus, although not intended for him alone, but for the universal Church. There are no other indications who this Theophilus was.

The purpose of Luke's writing was, as the Venerable Bede thinks, to offset the many apocryphal gospels that were being circulated then, such as gospels under the name of Thomas, Matthias, or the twelve Apostles.   Luke furnishes information, not given in the two previous Gospels, concerning the infancy and childhood of Christ and John the Baptist, the conversion of Mary Magdalen, Zaccheus, and one of the two thieves on the cross, the parable of the Pharisee and the Publican, of the lost sheep, of the prodigal son, showing forth especially the mercy of Christ towards sinners and suffering humanity.

Luke is also the author of the Acts of the Apostles, which have formed the basis of the history of the Primitive Church in the preceding chapters.

ST. JOHN

St. John wrote his Gospel in Greek, towards the end of his life, after his return from exile on Patmos. His chief purpose in writing it was to refute the rising heresies of Ebion and Cerinthus, who denied the divinity of Christ, and also to supply what the three other evangelists had omitted, as regards especially Christ's deeds in the first year of his public life. John the Evangelist is compared with the eagle, which in its flight attains greater heights than the other birds.   John alone treats professedly of the divinity of Christ, of the eternal birth of the Word, of eternity, of the procession and inspiration of the Holy Ghost. The Gospel of St. John concludes the written word of God, for in the order of its composition it is the last of the New Testament.

In 160 the four gospels were essentially as we now

read them; the autographs of the evangelists did not survive the early years of the Church.

In the Holy Bible we have three inspired epistles of St. John; there is no longer any doubt about their author.

In his first epistle he teaches us true faith, hope, and charity—Faith in the Holy Trinity and in the Incarnation, which he explains in his Gospel and in his epistles in a more sublime way than any of the inspired writers. He fills us with hope, while he reminds us of the love of the Father, who segregated us from the children of the devil, that we might be called and be in reality children of God. The whole letter breathes the most ardent love. In it at the same time he refutes the errors of those who denied the divinity of Christ or His real humanity; he rejects the error of those who claim that besides faith no other good works are necessary.

This letter was addressed like those of James, Peter and Jude to all the faithful. In the beginning of the letter John does not mention his name, as the other inspired letter writers generally do, with the exception of Paul in his letter to the Hebrews. John wrote these letters in his old age, as is clear from the terms he uses—calling himself the ancient and the faithful his little children, and justly so. He was by profession the oldest of all Christians; he was the last survivor of the Apostles.

His second letter was probably addressed to a lady named Electa. Some have thought that Electa may have been an epithet applied to a particular church, such as the chosen church of the Corinthians, which John salutes in the name of the chosen church of Ephesus. Others surmise that the Electas mentioned in the letter were sisters not by blood, but in spirit and in faith, disciples of the same master, probably of St. John himself. In either way, the instructions given by St. John are lessons to those especially who from their connections, situation, or condition in life are in danger of perversion.

John's third letter is addressed to one Gaius, perhaps the one whom we have met with Paul at Corinth. John praises him for his hospitality towards the faithful pilgrims and blames Diotrephis for just the reverse. He proclaims the praises of the first in his own name and in the name of all the faithful, and expresses the wish to meet him soon.

St. John also wrote the Apocalypse, the last book of the Bible. He composed it on the island of Patmos, to which he had been exiled under emperor Domitian, the successor of Titus, the destroyer of Jerusalem. It was written about 25 years after the destruction of the Holy City, in the year 97, two years before he wrote his Gospel and four years before his death.

There are many opinions concerning the subject matter of this prophetic book. Some think that it portrays the perpetual warfare between good and wicked and the final destiny of both. Others think with far more likelihood that it describes a few of the chief events affecting the Church in the course of ages, and especially at the end of the world.

The writer's purpose was to animate the faithful of his day and all others to constancy in suffering, at the sight of all the tortures under Domitian and other persecutors to follow. He warns them to be mindful of the glory of the Martyrs, the Virgins, and all the Blessed, and of the eternal damnation of the wicked.

When John was at Patmos, many heresies and abuses had arisen in the churches of Asia. In his Apocalypse as in his Gospel he corrects these abuses and shows the absurdity of heresy.

The Apocalypse is of all the books of Holy Scripture the most obscure and the hardest to explain, because it is full of symbols and enigmas, and because its prophecies have not yet been fulfilled.

ST. PAUL

The Acts of the Apostles are for the greater part concerned with the apostolic labors of St. Paul, and form the inspired history of the Primitive Church. Paul was not only a great preacher but also a great writer. In the Bible we have 14 of his epistles. It is most likely that one or more have been lost. These epistles treat both of faith and of morals. The first part of nearly all is dogmatic and concerns questions of faith; the second part is ethical and concerns the morals of the faithful. All mysteries of faith may be found in these letters. He insists chiefly upon the divine economy of grace and proves that Christ is our only Redeemer, from Whom we must beg and expect every grace, all justice, and life eternal. Then he shows that all Jewish ceremonies have been abrogated by the law of Christ. Finally he warns all to beware of heresy, which at that early period, began to sprout. Paul and all the other Apostles had been sent by Christ to promulgate, explain and inculcate whatever concerned redemption and salvation, all things unknown to the world but necessary for all. He combated especially the Jewish works and ceremonies, that were not Christian, as in his epistles to the Romans, the Galatians, the Philippians and the Hebrews. In the others he uproots rising heresies, such as of Simon the Magician, Menander, the Gnostics and others, who were also exposed by Jude and Peter in his second epistle. In his remaining epistles he instructs those whom he addresses, solves their doubts, perfects, and confirms them in Christian faith and practice.

All these letters are filled with gems of wisdom and practical guidance. The heresies we mentioned above were contemporary with the Apostles; from the beginning the enemy sowed cockle in the wheat.

In the second part of these epistles Paul teaches Christian virtues and Christian ethics, not in a continuous treatise, but in brief sentences. This was the custom with inspired writers of the Old Testament, as we see in Proverbs, Ecclesiastes and Ecclesiasticus, and also with the Greek pagan writers of that time.

The epistles of St. Paul seem to have been written in the following order—1 Thessalonians, 2 Thessalonians, 1 Corinthians, 1 Timothy, 2 Corinthians,

Galatians, Romans, Titus, 2 Timothy, Ephesians, Philippians, Colossians, Philemon, Hebrews.

The last six of these were written, while Paul was a prisoner in Rome.

ST. JAMES

The writer of this epistle is James the Less, as distinguished from the Apostle of Spain, because he was younger, or called later, or for some other reason. He is called the brother of the Lord, but not in the ordinary acceptation of the term. James had two brothers among the Apostles—Jude and Simon. He was a minister of the circumcision, because he preached to the Jews only. He was the first bishop of Jerusalem. The Venerable Bede thinks that he was so appointed on the day following the martydom of St. Stephen, to calm the animosity of the Jews for the severe rebuke that had fallen from the lips of the proto-martyr. Paul calls him a pillar of the Church with Peter (Gal. II.9). Peter delivered from prison sent without delay a messenger to James (Acts XII.17). Jude glories in the fact that he is a brother of James. On account of the prominence of this son, his mother is called the mother of James, although she had three other sons, and two of these among the Apostles.

James was the real protector of the Jews. To win them and lead them to Christ, he kept the law so long as it could conscientiously be kept; he advised Paul to adopt the same course in order to provide for his safety and their conversion. The early writers call attention to the physical resemblance of James to his divine Master, and so explain why Judas gave the particular sign to the Jews for fear that the one might be mistaken for the other. James' life on earth was a reflexion of the life of the Blessed in heaven. He was present at the first council in Jerusalem. He was martyred probably during the seventh year of Nero. There is a great difference of opinions concerning his age at the time of his death. Some place it at 96, but it seems improbable that Christ should have selected a septuagenarian for the arduous duties of the apostolate; all the others were young when called.

Eusebius the historian gives us the following description of his life, martyrdom, and death: James was a saint from birth, he drank no wine or beer, and abstained from fleshmeat; he never shaved his head. He alone was allowed to enter into the Holy of Holies. Assiduousness in prayer on his knees had so hardened them as to resemble those of a camel. James was so loved by the Jews that, after having witnessed his zeal for their conversion, they approached him with a request that he stop the losses in their ranks. James seized the last occasion to speak to them about his Master. His frank and open profession of faith cost him his life. After being precipitated from the pinnacle of the temple, and landing nearly dead, he begged God with eyes raised to heaven to forgive them. James had also been favored by a special apparition of Christ after His resurrection.

The purpose of James in writing his epistle was, first, to animate the faithful to constancy in the midst of the persecution, which they endured both from Jews and Gentiles; and secondly, to commend good works and the practice of virtues, of piety and charity in particular. In 'it he teaches us that all evil proceeds from us, and that all good comes from God; he distinguishes heavenly from earthly wisdom; he declares that the world is inimical to God, and God to the world; he insists that we mortify concupiscence, that God is the judge and avenger of all; that we must seek God's friendship in preference to that of the world; he condemns overanxiety concerning the future and recommends implicit confidence in God's providence. James left us in his epistle the clear statement that one of the means devised by Christ to pour out his graces is the anointment of the sick.

This letter was written shortly before the death of the Apostle. The Apostles were all so intent upon preaching the word of God, that only in the later years of their life they conveyed some of their teaching in writing. Unlike the letters of Paul, this epistle was addressed to the universal Church.

ST. PETER

Of St. Peter we have two epistles. The first of these was written in Rome in the year that Peter moved his episcopal see from Antioch to the Eternal

City, and was sent by Sylvanus to the faithful at Antioch. The proof is that Mark was still with Peter, as he sent Mark's greetings; Peter sent him that year to preside over the church of Alexandria, after Mark had already written his Gospel in Rome.

It was addressed primarily to the converted Jews, dispersed over Pontus, Galatia, Cappadocia, Asia and Bithynia, as the title indicates, for these were the original converts of Peter, and of these he took special care, but secondarily also to the converted Gentiles, because as Chief Pastor of the Church he was interested in all.

Peter argues in his letter about faith and morals. In regard to faith he shows the wonderful counsel of God, and the blessing of the Incarnation, Passion, and Redemption, and the call of the Jews and of the Gentiles to faith and glory. He upholds the right doctrine, foretold by the prophets, and preached by the Apostles at the command of God, which we must constantly follow, and for which we must be prepared to sacrifice our very lives. Thence he passes to morals. He teaches the faithful obedience to the temporal rulers, even if they be pagans. He shows the conscientious relations between masters and servants, husbands and wives, young and old, faithful and spiritual leaders. In the recommendation of virtues he lays special stress upon patience in tribulation.

The same teaching is also found in the epistles of Paul, James, and Jude. They were all moved by the same Holy Ghost to record the same truths; all thought and expressed themselves in the same way concerning the virtues of a Christian; all adopted the same norm in teaching sound Christian morality.

There is a great difference of style and phraseology between the two epistles of Peter; he had probably a different secretary for each. The second letter was written towards the end of his life. It is the message of a father about to say farewell to the Church on earth and to the world; he warns his children against false teachers and scoffers, and tells them of the sudden dissolution of the world.

Incidentally he remarks that even in Scripture, viz., in the epistles of Paul, there are certain things hard to understand, which the unwise might take to their own destruction, intimating the need of interpreters of the revealed word.

Peter passed the last nine months of his life in the Mamertine prison; there he found leisure to instruct by letter those that he could no longer address personally; thus was the second letter written from his prison.

ST. JUDE

There were two men by the name of Judas in the apostolic college—Judas Iscariot and Judas the brother of James. His mother was a cousin of the Blessed Virgin. She had four sons, three of whom were called to the apostolate—James, Jude, and Simon, and the fourth, Joseph, was one of the two candidates at the election of the traitor's successor.

All are called brothers of Christ, that is, relatives of Christ. Jude was also named Thaddeus. Although evangelizing Persia, he wrote his epistle in Greek and addressed it to the universal Church. As Origen says, the epistle is very short, it contains only 25 verses, but it is full of heavenly wisdom. This short epistle confirms explicitly many points concerning faith. In a dogmatic way we find in it the mystery of the Most Holy Trinity, the difference between good and bad angels, belief in and fear of the last judgment.

Its moral teaching embraces abhorrence of impurity, blasphemy and other capital vices, also constancy in prayer, charity in the conversion of the erring, and of heretics, and praise of God. It is a compendium of the whole theology,—a gospel all in one chapter.

The purpose of Jude was to crush the heresies then existing, such as of Simon the Magician, of Cerinthus, and of the Nichoalites, and others that would soon be born from them. He warns his readers against the consequences of this aberration from truth, and teaches them constancy in the faith, lest they suffer like the Sodomites and the apostate angels, who all perished miserably.

This epistle is a standing condemnation of heresy; the faithful must fight it, if they would not perish with the rebels. He compares these heretics to Cain, Balaam, and Core, and calls them: clouds without water, trees of the autumn, raging waves of the sea, wandering stars. He tells us ever to be faithful to the teaching of the Apostles and to resist the false prophets; he also suggests the means to be preserved from error, and bring back those that have seceded.

This epistle and the second of St. Peter confirm each other; there is no absolute certainty as to which was written first.

CHAPTER TWENTY-SEVENTH

THE SUCCESSORS OF ST. PETER UP TO THE END
OF THE FIRST CENTURY

THE first visible head of the Church after Christ had been put to death like his Master, by crucifixion. As the Church was to continue as a visible society up to the end of time, the mantle of Peter's authority and primacy had to fall on other shoulders. At the time of his death some of the other Apostles may have been living; St. John certainly was. None of them came to Rome to claim the succession.

Eusebius and other ancient writers inform us that the first to receive the episcopate of the Roman Church after the martyrdom of Peter and Paul was Linus. Paul mentioned his name in the second letter he wrote from Rome to Timothy; among others he sent to his disciple the greetings of Linus. From authentic sources we gather the following details of his life and of his pontificate. He hailed from Volterra, and was therefore an Italian by birth. He ruled the Church for 11 years and 3 months. Most probably he assisted Peter in the government of the Church, and by his command he established that women should have the head veiled, when entering the church. Ancient writers also tell us that Linus condemned the followers of Menander, who was a disciple of Simon the Magician, and officially declared that the God of the Old Testament is the Creator of all, and that there is nothing wrong in the nature of things.

The destruction of Jerusalem occurred under the pontificate of Linus, and together with the triumph of the Roman forces over the Jews under Vespasian and Titus, and the verification of Christ's prophecy concerning the Holy City. Linus is venerated as a martyr, although under his pontificate there was no general persecution against the Church; the fact shows that Linus suffered great hardships for the faith. In the public liturgy his name comes immediately after those of the Apostles, which proves his great merits and his holiness. He was buried near the tomb of St. Peter. At the time of the restoration of St. Peter's basilica a sarcophagus was found bearing the simple inscription—"Linus."

Some ancient writers have thought that the first successor of Peter was not Linus but Clement. The reason perhaps of their belief was that in a letter to St. James, Clement asserts that he was consecrated bishop by St. Peter. Although such apocryphal writings, owing to their antiquity, carry some weight, yet they do not offset the testimony of so many others. The consecration may be quite correct, and further it may be true that in his humility he twice refused the succession, and thus enabled Linus and Cletus to succeed the one after the other. Most likely not only Clement, but also Linus and Cletus were consecrated bishops by St. Peter, to be his helpers in those terrible days, especially when duty forced upon him long absences from the city.

The second successor from 78 to 90 was St. Cletus. He was a Roman, and governed the Church 12 years, 1 month and 11 days. He lived in the days of Vespasian and Titus. He carried out a command of Blessed Peter by ordaining 25 priests for Rome. It is hard to determine the number of Christians at that time in Rome. We know from an official document that in 252 there were 44 priests for about 50,000 Christians; this estimate is probably too low. The number of 25 priests under Cletus indicates at any rate that Christianity had made considerable progress. Cletus was buried on the Vatican Hill near the body of St. Peter. The oldest documents give us that information.

In some old catalogues one Anacletus is mentioned as an occupant of St. Peter's chair, and this has led to the controversy whether he was with Cletus one and the same person. Anacletus is said to have been a Greek from Athens and to have lived in the days of Domitian. Without settling the question we would remark that the most ancient Fathers and writers name only one between Linus and Clement, and that is Cletus. The Annuario published at the Vatican gives Anacletus as Clement's successor.

Clement succeeded Cletus. St. Irenæus writes about him as follows: Clement was the third from Peter to occupy the episcopal chair. He had seen the Apostles and conversed with them, but he was not the only one; many others instructed by the Apostles still survived.

Under the pontificate of Clement a great dissension arose among the brethren at Corinth. He wrote to the Corinthians a very important letter, in which he invited them to peace among themselves, strengthened their faith, and told them what traditions they had recently received from the Apostles. There is no doubt about the genuineness of this letter; of other letters to the Corinthians and to his brothers, we are not so sure. To understand the nature of his undoubtedly genuine letter to the Corinthians we must remark that indeed great trouble existed in that church. Priests appointed by the Apostles or by their successors and known for their integrity of life and their learning were driven out or deposed. This happened when St. John was still among the living and several years before his death. Yet the better element among the Corinthians looked for a remedy in those desperate circumstances, not to St. John, but to the occupant of Peter's chair. Modern writers think that this letter was written in 97 towards the end of Domitian's persecution. In it Clement recalled to the Corinthians the former high reputation of their church, its piety and hospitality, its obedience and discipline. Jealousy had brought about the trouble; he urged them to repent and to preserve order as all creation does. He warned them that the Apostles had provided a succession of pastors, that could not be removed at will. Clement concluded by stating that he would be happy, if they would obey. He sent two venerable messengers to show how great his anxiety for peace was; he hoped that they would soon return bearers of a favorable report.

Clement was a Roman by birth.   According to a Roman tradition, he came from a noble family related to Vespasian, and was a relative also of the consul Flavius Clemens, who under Domitian with his wife Flavia Domitilla was arrested for his faith. It is further claimed that the site of the present church of St. Clement was that of his father's house. Clement divided the city into seven regions, which he committed to seven notaries, whose duty was to compile carefully the acts of the martyrs.

In Clement's time the second general persecution against the Christians arose, in the later days of emperor Domitian.   After the death of Nero in June, 68, Galba, Otho, and Vitellius contested the throne, but in a short time all perished miserably.   In December, 69, Vespasian came into possession; he was succeeded in 79 by Titus, who died in September, 81. The next occupant was Domitian, Titus' younger brother; he was a real pervert and reigned up to 96, when he was killed. His successors were Nerva (96–98) and Trajan (98–117).

In the third year of Trajan, that is, in the year 100, Clement was sent in exile to the Crimea, and cast into the sea.

CHAPTER TWENTY-EIGHTH

THE DESTRUCTION OF JERUSALEM

JUDAISM in the designs of Providence had served its purpose in the history of the world as a preparation for Christianity. Jerusalem and its temple, the center of Jewish worship, no longer had their primitive importance; they could no longer exist without harm to Christianity, which they menaced with a double danger—confusion of doctrine and persecution. The Christian converts from Judaism would have been the principal victims; they were exposed to the hatred of their former coreligionists, and they themselves would foment division within the ranks of the Church against the converts from paganism, or make a mixture of discordant elements. The destruction of Jerusalem and of its temple was therefore an event of the highest importance for the diffusion of Christianity, as the Saviour Himself had foretold, when both city and temple were at the height of their glory and magnificence. The Jews had been the chosen instruments in the designs of God's providence, and still clung to prerogatives, which they had lost. The most touching marks of God's mercy, the past and impending chastisements, had failed to open the eyes of the stiff-necked people

to the light of God's revelation. They had inter-
preted the prophecies concerning the Messiah in a
narrow political way, and failed to recognize in Jesus
of Nazareth the long expected Messiah.   The Roman
domination upset all their calculations, when it
should have proved the fulfilment of Jacob's prophecy.   A crisis was imminent.

Oppressed by the Roman governors at Cæsarea,
the Jews meditated revenge and they openly revolted
under the governorship of Gestius Florus.   The near
occasion of the revolt was the sacrifice of some birds
by a pagan near the synagogue in derision of Jewish
worship.   The revolt soon spread to Jerusalem, and
in 67 the whole nation rose against Rome.   The terrible day was near, when the Saviour's prophecy
would be fulfilled to the letter.

Nero charged Vespasian with the high command
of the Roman forces.   Vespasian, whom Titus joined
on his return from Egypt, invaded Galilee with a
powerful army.   After an obstinate resistance of 40
days on the part of the Jews, he captured the
strongest fortress they had in that province; the
battle cost the lives of thousands of Jews; after that
the general easily subdued the whole province.   The
victorious armies were most anxious to continue their
triumphal march into Judea, to take and destroy
Jerusalem and so end the war.   The prudent leader
waited for a favorable moment, which the internal
divisions among the Jews would hasten.

The older men of Judea desired peace, but the
younger generation breathed hatred and war.   Ves-

pasian first subdued the rest of Judea and then camped in sight of Jerusalem in the spring of 68. Nero had killed himself, after having been declared a traitor to the empire by the Roman senate. Vespasian awaited orders from his successor. The Roman army proclaimed Vespasian emperor, who then entrusted his son Titus with the task to conclude the victorious war. We borrow the following details from Josephus, the great Jewish historian of this war.

Fearful signs had appeared in Jerusalem as forebodings of imminent disaster. Fiery armies had been noticed moving about in the air; a great light shone near the altar; the bronze east door of the temple had opened by itself; a mysterious voice had been heard in the temple saying: Let us move hence. Titus had arrived from Cæsarea with new forces to besiege the city. The Christians in the besieged city remembered the prophecy of their Master; "When you shall see Jerusalem compassed about with an army, then know that the desolation thereof is at hand" (Luke XXI.20). They left the city in company with their bishop, St. Simeon, the successor of St. James, and moved to Pella across the Jordan. Josephus Flavius tells us that the Jews foreseeing what was going to happen, brought into the city such an abundance of provisions that they could have carried on the war for several years. The various factions in their hatred of one another practically destroyed all in five months, from April to September, with the result that a horrible famine prevailed. They defended themselves behind embankments of dead bodies, which soon caused pest.

Titus arrived at Easter, when an immense multitude had been attracted to the city for the Pasch. Josephus estimated it at 2,700,000, but Tacitus only mentions 600,000. The defenders of the city, after having fought the common enemy, began to murder one another. They were all witnesses of the fulfilment of a prophecy of the Nazarean, whom they had mocked. With pest, famine, beastly hatred, sedition and murder, the abomination of desolation had come. A mother unable to feed her child would kill it, roast its flesh, eat some, and give the rest to the hungry crowd. The news of these horrors soon spread to the camp of the Romans, who were so horrified that they decided to bury these horrors under the ruins of Jerusalem. In vain did Titus invite the besieged to surrender; the Romans then stormed the city and took it by assault. A soldier put fire to the temple; it burnt down. The whole city was wiped out and levelled to the ground. During the war over a million people perished, and 97,000 were taken prisoners and sold as slaves elsewhere.

The Jews had lost their nationality; they were scattered all over the world. No promise of restoration! no more prophets or kings! no altar! no temple! The scepter had departed for ever from Juda!

The scattered Jews and Christians soon after were allowed to return to the devastated city; the faithful with their bishop returned; their ranks were increased with the accession of numerous Jews.

About 250 years later a Roman emperor named

Julian (the Apostate) tried to pass the lie on the Nazarean and all His prophecies concerning the destruction of the temple. When young, Julian had as fellow student on the school benches of Athens, Gregory of Nazianzum. The future saint and doctor of the Church prophetically said of the future emperor: "What a monster the Roman empire raises in its bosom!" Julian induced the Jews to rebuild the temple and helped them with his money. But his efforts were in vain. The first attempt was frustrated by fire emerging from the foundations; earthquakes and other signs destroyed all the material brought together for the construction. The incident is related by a pagan writer. A second attempt had equally to be abandoned. Since then the Jews never tried to rebuild the temple, although humanly speaking with the means at their disposal, it would have been an easy undertaking.

CHAPTER TWENTY-NINTH

HERESIES OF THE FIRST CENTURY

Besides the external wars or persecutions, the Church experienced from the beginning internal wars —heresies and schisms, but as history records, she came out victorious over the one and the other variety.

The standardbearer of heresy in the days of the Apostles was Simon the Magician, with whom we became acquainted at Samaria, when after his baptism by Philip, the deacon, he saw the wonderful results of the imposition of the hands of the Apostles on the neophytes. He tried then to buy from Peter and John the privilege of giving the Holy Ghost. Not all need be admitted that great writers, like Justin the Philosopher, Irenæus, Tertullian and Eusebius have left us about him. Whether it is absolutely correct that he had his statue among the gods of Rome, learned modern critics argue among themselves; whether he had his statue on the Tiberine island, between the two bridges, with the dedicatory inscription: To Simon the holy god; and whether this statue is the same as that found in 1574 in that neighborhood, is immaterial. Many learned critics uphold St. Justin, who gives us further details of Simon's teaching.

Simon gave himself out as a quasi-god; under Claudius he came to the imperial city of Rome, where for his magic he was looked upon as god; many of the Samaritans and many of other nations worshipped him as a god of the first order. Helen an infamous woman, who was his steady companion, was considered as the mother of all other beings. In Rome he addressed the senate and the people, who gave him a place among the gods. St. Augustin tells us that he gave out pictures of himself and his companion, to be adored by his disciples. St. Irenæus speaks of the advent of Simon in Rome, as of an historical fact beyond question. As Simon could not make headway in Samaria, no wonder that he went to the city, to which, according to Tacitus, all that was atrocious and infamous flocked and was in honor. Another writer, Arnobius, who wrote towards the end of the third century, informs us that when Simon was reminded of his old age he guaranteed to rise the third day, if he were buried. He ordered his disciples to dig a grave and to bury him. They carried out the command, but he remained there up to the present, because he was not the Christ, says Arnobius. What the Fathers and other sacred writers of a later date relate of Simon and of his violent death cannot simply be called a myth. If it is doubtful whether the narrative of Simon's flight and of his crash to the earth is fiction; so long as no proofs are given to the contrary, we prefer to believe the evidence of the above named great writers and to admit that Peter's prayer brought down the impostor. Simon's crash ended his life and his glory.

The Gnostics were the most famous of the heretics, who in the beginning of the Church corrupted the teaching of Christ with pernicious errors. They were so called because they boasted a true knowledge of God and of things divine. Gnosticism, one of the religio-political theories in vogue even before Christ, and spread over the Orient, was born of pride preventing the human mind from renouncing ideas in opposition to divine revelation. The Gnostics considered matter as the source of all evil, and therefore claimed that it could not have been created by a good God, that it was eternal, and that some spirits had created from it the world and men. Good spirits of different sex had been created by God, and from their union other spirits proceeded, but less perfect; each successive generation implied a gradual deterioration. One of the lower order of spirits had created this world from vicious matter; he successfully resisted all the influences of a superior order, but eventually he will fall through the power of another spirit to be sent to men. Many Gnostics considered Christ to be that spirit and were baptized; others endeavored to conciliate their principles with the Christian doctrine and hideously corrupted it. This and other heresies of that time differed one from another under some respects, but agreed under other. All denied that Christ was true God; all claimed that he assumed not a real but an ethereal body, or simply the shadow of a body, and therefore did not truly suffer and die.   They all rejected the Old Testament in so far as the creation of the world by God is concerned; of the New Testament they rejected all that was contrary to their views.   We have related in the preceding chapters the arguments of St. Paul with them and remarked that the Apostles in their writings warned the faithful against them.

The Judaizers were converted Jews, who in the early days still clung to the Mosaic ritual.   These Christians admitted besides Christ another source of spiritual life, the law of Moses, and therefore threw a doubt upon the divinity of Christ.   Eventually they separated from the Church and formed a separate sect.   This sect split into two; some sided with Peter and observed the law without making salvation depend upon it; others pretended that the observance of the law was binding on all, on converts from paganism as well as on converts from Judaism.   The latter caused considerable agitation in the church of Antioch about the year 50, and later on in Galatia and at Corinth.   At the death of St. James the Judaizers had their candidate for the see of Jerusalem, but he was not elected and St. Simeon took the place of the martyred Apostle.   This led to the first formal schism.   During the siege of Jerusalem the Judaizers separated entirely from the Christian body and with the Esseneans formed the sect of the Ebionites.   With them Christ was a mere man born according to the laws of nature.   The Apostle of the Gentiles was to them the object of a deepseated hatred; he was an apostate. They accepted as a source of religious information the Hebrew version of the Gospel of St. Matthew only. Their leader Ebion with some others gave to their creed the appearance of a theosophic asceticism.

Advanced systems of philosophy menaced the Church more than the crude pretensions of Judaism. The deceitful reasonings of Greek and Oriental philosopy, especially those of Philo, mixed with Christian truth tended to deprive the latter of its divine character. In their disregard for matter these philosophers had adopted the theory of dualism and emanation, and were very active at Colossus, Ephesus, and in Greece and gained followers among the Pharisees of Palestine. Their chief, Menander, gave himself out for the Messiah, and therefore St. Irenæus calls him the successor of Simon the Magician. He claimed for himself divine power, which put him above the angels, and his special mission was to deliver the world of them. He introduced the rite of baptism among his followers.

St. Irenæus tells us that Cerinthus was a contemporary of St. John; he was one of the strictest Judaizers. His doctrine was a mixture of Christianity and Judaism. He admitted a supreme God, a mysterious being without any relation to the visible world; he thought the world created by a being inferior to the supreme God, what the Jews adored under the name of Jehovah was only an angel. Jesus was for him like for the Ebionites remarkable for His wisdom and His piety; at His baptism the supreme Logos came down upon Him and filled His soul; He had revealed the Father unknown up to then; He performed miracles, but the Logos left Jesus, and the man alone suffered and rose again; the Logos could not suffer.   Cerinthus and his followers admitted only the Gospel of St. Matthew; they hated above all the writings of St. Paul and of St. John.   Eusebius narrates that Cerinthus wrote a book in opposition to St. John; he called it inspired as also all his other erroneous ideas, and named it his apocalypse.   He thought like the Jews generally that the Messiah would establish on earth a material and glorious kingdom, and was a precursor of Millenarianism wrongly understood.

The teaching of the Nicolaites was a mixture of the ideas of Cerinthus with Gnosticism.   Whether their leader was Nicholas, one of the seven deacons, or simply borrowed his name, is not clear.   Ancient writers credit him with the grossest immorality.   It is probable that those reproved by St. Peter (II.151) and by St. Jude (2–21) were the Nicolaites, and that after the departure and death of St. Paul they gained ground in Asia Minor.   This constrained St. John shortly after the death of Peter and Paul to return to Ephesus and lead a vigorous campaign against them.

The enemy of all good realized that the power of the Cross would cause the idols to crumble; he then tried heresy and schism to supplant faith, corrupt truth, and destroy unity.   The snares of the devil were numerous from the very beginning; we need not wonder if these early would-be reformers have their followers in all subsequent ages. Christ had guaranteed the stability of His Church against all assaults and vicissitudes. To offset the evil effects of heresy and schism, to remove the cockle from the wheat, God selected the Apostle of love, the last survivor of the twelve. He combated heresy not only by word, but also by his Gospel, the most sublime model of true contemplation and mysticism, and by his first epistle, which is as a preface to his Gospel. But we need not look in this controversy for an open fight against the heretics. St. John refutes heresy by the exposition of the truth, as did his disciple Ignatius after him. So are all the above heresies victoriously refuted, especially in the first chapter of John's Gospel. The Logos who created all and without whom nothing is created is not merely a human being, nor a God inferior to the Father, but the co-eternal and consubstantial Son of God, who became man. Not by the Mosaic Law is admission granted to the society of the Logos, but by the faith in Christ.

John unfolds in his Apocalypse the destinies of the Church, always victorious over all revolutions that shall shake it up to the day, when this world shall be renewed, until this earthly Jerusalem shall have been transformed into the heavenly city. That apostolic zeal for all wayward children of the Church, so transparent in his Gospel and in his epistles, did not grow weaker through the weight of years for the centenarian Apostle.

CHAPTER THIRTIETH

PUBLIC WORSHIP IN THE DAYS OF THE APOSTLES

THE public worship or the Liturgy, which is a certain arrangement of prayers and ceremonies, as we have it to-day, did not exist in the days of the Apostles. The mystical breaking of the bread or the Eucharistic service had not an altogether set formula, but was partly composed by the officiating bishop or priest. The ceremonial gradually grew out of certain obvious actions, sometimes performed for convenience sake only; in a similar way developed the church vestments. But all actions and all ceremonies of the Liturgy were not left to the improvisation of the officiating minister; a considerable liberty left to him in that regard explains the absence of absolute unity in the early Christian churches.

In regard to the public worship *par excellence*— the celebration of the Holy Eucharist—we find from the very beginning a uniform nucleus founded upon what Christ Himself had done at the Last Supper. In the Primitive Church we find much more than the essential part in the celebration. Lessons, psalms, prayer, and preaching preceded; this was a continuation of the service of the synagogue; Amen was retained.

Two early ceremonies, that accompanied the celebration, soon disappeared; they were not essential. The first was the love-feast; the other the spiritual exercises, in which people were moved by the Holy Ghost to prophesy, speak in divers tongues, heal the sick by prayer, and so on; St. Paul in his first epistle to the Corinthians refers to that (XVI.1–14). Apart from the account of the Last Supper we find in the New Testament various other liturgical forms, such as the following: reading of the sacred books, sermons, psalms, and hymns, public liturgical prayers for all classes of people, the faithful lifted up their hands at prayer, men with uncovered heads, women with heads veiled; kiss of peace; there was an offertory of goods for the poor, and this received the special name of communion. In his first epistle to the Corinthians St. Paul shows that to the first Christians the table of the Eucharist was an altar; in the Acts (XX.11) he breaks bread, communicates, and preaches. From this nucleus gradually developed the liturgy of later ages. The center of religious worship now is the Holy Eucharist and the real presence. It is interesting to know what the great Apostle of the Gentiles thought about it.

In his first epistle to the Corinthians (XI.23 and foll.) St. Paul presents the Eucharistic doctrine, not as something new to the people, but as well known. He recalls to their mind what they do believe in order to excite them to greater devotion. His arguments, when taken in their entirety, illustrate the certainty of the Apostle's mind. How he received of the Lord his Eucharistic narrative, whether directly or indirectly, he does not openly say, but we may admit that he learned the words and the actions from the Apostles. Christ could have taught him directly, but he could also teach him through the Apostles, as He did concerning His Resurrection.

In regard to the sacrifice, he speaks of the body of the Lord that shall be delivered for you; it is Christ in the form of a victim; and by adding after both sacrificial sentences of Christ the words: "Do this for a commemoration of me" he does not appeal to the bloody sacrifice of the cross. The words of Christ, as repeated by St. Paul—"This chalice is the New Testament in my blood"—remind us of the Old Testament, which Moses consecrated by sprinkling the sacrificed blood upon the people (Ex. XXIV.8). Christ, in order to confirm in a more wonderful way the New Testament, does not sprinkle the sacrificed blood upon the people, but gives it to them to drink. The Apostles were commanded to do what Christ had done; therefore they also must produce the body and blood of Christ in a sacrificial state; unless they did so, it does not appear how they would announce the death of the Lord; the eating of it only does not represent death.

In the previous chapter of the same epistle (X.21) he wrote: "You cannot be partakers of the table of the Lord and of the table of devils." There is no doubt but that the table of devils meant sacrifice; the context makes that very plain; as an evident parallelism, the table of the Lord also means sacrifice. The above words are taken from Malachy (I.7–12), where the prophet certainly treats of sacrifices. In that same prophecy we find that splendid promise of a future sacrifice. No doubt therefore is possible; Paul opposed the Eucharistic sacrifice to the pagan sacrifices. In his letter to the Hebrews (XIII.10) Paul says: "We have an altar, whereof they have no power to eat who serve the tabernacle." The objection from the same epistle to the effect that the sacrifice of the cross is sufficient for all, falls, when we consider that St. Paul never claimed that the Eucharistic sacrifice was essentially different from that of the cross. The assertion that the sacrifice of praise (Psalm 40) as nowadays misunderstood, is all that is required is equally absurd. The sacrifice of praise in that psalm is not praise without a sacrifice, but sacrifice with praise. Moreover, if it were to be taken in a metaphorical sense, why are not the Jews allowed to offer it?

As Paul believed in a true sacrifice of the body and blood of Christ, so he believed in the real presence under the sacramental veil. He repeats the words of institution without any explanation, to inspire the Corinthians with greater respect. He would have missed his purpose entirely if they could have objected that all was to be understood metaphorically. Paul could not have expressed himself more clearly than when he judged guilty of the body and blood of Christ those who receive the Eucharist unworthily (1 Cor. XI.27). In verse 29 he tells us that the like eat and drink judgment to themselves, if they do not consider that Eucharistic body as the body of Christ. In the preceding chapter (X.16–17) he states just as plainly his belief, and he further shows that as we all partake of one bread, that Eucharistic bread is not transformed in us, but we are transformed into it to become one bread. There would not be one bread, if it were not one body of Christ. Through that communion the divine life received in baptism is nourished; it effects that Christ lives in us (Gal. II.20) and through it we are all one in Christ (III.28).

Our Lord very likely instituted the Eucharist after the ordinary supper, and the early Christians seem to have had their Eucharistic celebration after the ordinary meal. When writing to the Corinthians (1 Cor. X.21–22) Paul seems to reprimand them for taking ordinary food before receiving the Holy Eucharist. It appears that the practice, introduced from Jerusalem was not countenanced by him, and that he abrogated it, but there is no certainty about it.

The teaching of St. Paul on that point was the teaching of all the Apostles, because faith is one; God the unchangeable truth, could not reveal one thing to Paul and the opposite to others.

What is true of the sacrifice of the New Law and of the real presence is just as true about all essentials of religion, and of the other means instituted by Christ for our salvation.

Kaufman in his "Manual of Christian Archæology" gives us the topography of some of the ancient Christian monuments of the first century. At Philippi may be seen the ruins of a church with a cupola in the form of a cross; at Corinth, Crete, Antioch, Damascus, Tyre, etc., there were in the first century churches worthy of the name.

The inspired word and authentic tradition have left us some interesting details of churches in Rome of apostolic origin. The Christian faith had probably been brought to the capital of the Cæsars by the strangers of Rome, who were in Peter's audience on the first Christian Pentecost and were converted by him. Among the very first apostles of Rome were some of the Italian band in garrison at Cæsarea, who were converted together with their centurion, Cornelius. Peter came shortly afterwards to Rome to organize that primitive Church. It was left in peace until 49, when, owing to frequent disturbances caused by the Jews, emperor Claudius drove all the adherents of the synagogue out of Rome. Many converts from Judaism in the confusion were exiled with them. Among these were Aquila with his wife Prisca or Priscilla, who eventually established themselves in Corinth, where Paul found them. They afterwards followed the Apostle to Ephesus, and they returned to Rome in the beginning of Nero's reign and certainly were there in 58. Both in his first letter to the Corinthians (XVI.19) and in his letter to the Romans (XVI.5) Paul mentions the church, which was in their house. From the greetings in Paul's letters we may form an idea of the importance of the Christian community in Rome at that time. Entire families had embraced the faith, and there were several churches in private houses.   One of these was in the house of Aquila and Prisca, on the Aventine, where now the church of St. Prisca stands.   There was a similar one on the Viminal, where the church of St. Pudenziana now is.   Much has been written about these two churches and their relations to the Apostles, but all is not equally clear.   The best authorities admit that the latter was originally the house of Pudens.   At the end of the fourth century, the priest in charge of this titular church caused to be reproduced in Mosaic for the same church the figure of Peter sitting on a chair and surrounded by the lambs of Christ—an allegorical allusion to the words of Christ: "Feed my lambs."   This shows that at the time it was a common tradition that Peter had really gathered the faithful at that place to teach them the heavenly doctrine.   In the second century, St. Justin the philosopher, certifies that he twice dwelt in that same place.

In regard to the other title of St. Prisca on the Aventine, which was the domestic church mentioned by St. Paul, it is said that Peter baptized there. The famous archæologist De Rossi suspected that there existed a relationship between the two churches or titles; this was afterwards confirmed by inscriptions found near this church.

From the very beginning the Christians had their own cemeteries, known under the name of their original owners, such as: Lucina, Priscilla, Callixtus, etc. The oldest of the catacombs or cemeteries belong to the first century.   The first was probably that of

Priscilla, the model of all. According to ancient documents the bodies of many saints and among them those of Pudenziana and Praxedis, daughters of Pudens, and contemporaries of the Apostles, rested there, as also Aquila and Prisca, the proprietors of the domestic church on the Aventine. Inscriptions in marble have preserved the memory of the couple, so dear to St. Paul. The fact that the characters on the tombstones are similar to those on the walls of Pompeii show that they belong to the first century. A visit among these venerable tombs of the first century gives us the sweet impression of attendance at the meetings of the faithful of the apostolic age.

In these domestic churches and cemeteries we find mural paintings of great interest. The most famous is that of the Madonna with the Child, which according to the unanimous verdict of archæologists belongs to the first half of the second century. This shows that veneration of the Mother of God is as old as the Church; the first Christians had heard from the lips of the dying Saviour the words: "Behold thy mother." It could not be expressed, however, in a public and solemn manner in those days of persecution. In the beginning to convert the heathen world the Christians studiously avoided whatever might cause a confusion between the spirituality of their religion with the superstitious practices of paganism. This explains the scarcity of images at that time. Christ Himself was nearly always represented under a symbolic form or as an historic person in the evangelical episodes; we need not wonder that the same happened in regard to His Mother. There are, however, now representations of the Virgin, dating from the days of the great persecutions and proving that the belief of the Christians on that point then was what it is to-day. One of these mural paintings represents the Virgin with the Infant and one of the Magi and the star. By comparison archæologists have come to the conclusion that this dates, from not later than the first half of the second century, and perhaps from the end of the first. As this was found near the cemetery of Priscilla, where the Apostles held forth, we may conclude that the painter had gathered precious information about the Mother of God from the Apostles themselves.

Besides the above there are other important monuments, but historically not so certain. We will mention only a few.

According to tradition the two Apostles were cast into a prison before their martyrdom. The name of Mamertine prison dates only from the Middle Ages. That common tradition does not contradict history or archæology; the two chambers, one above the other, were certainly the city prison in imperial days. Peter in jail converted his jailers, Processus and Martinian; he miraculously caused water to flow from a spring to baptize them. This tradition is traced back to the fifth or sixth century; it is certain that in the eighth century the place was held in great veneration. The spring of St. Peter, as it is called, may still be seen in the Mamertine prison.

In the same acts of Processus and Martinian, dating from the sixth century, a flight of St. Peter from prison is also recorded. On the way he is supposed to have lost a bandage used to bind up the wounds produced on his legs by the chains. This was picked up by a pious matron, who kept it and caused a church to be built in her house under the title of Fasciola or bandage. The document recording this is much posterior to the fact, but it is certain that this title is one of the most ancient and the most important; from it depended the great cemetery of Domitilla of very remote origin.

We are also told that St. Peter on his flight from the city, on the same Appian Way, a short distance from the walls, met Christ. Peter amazed asked him: "Lord, whither goest Thou?" Christ replied: "I go to Rome to be crucified again." Peter understood the lesson, returned to the city, and shortly afterwards was crucified. The oratory built on the spot is known under the name of "Quo Vadis." Many other details that have gradually grown around these episodes do not deserve credence.

Other ancient documents record the spot, where Simon the Magician crashed to earth at the prayer of St. Peter. This tradition is traced back to the third century, and was commonly admitted in the fourth.

There are numerous other places recording events connected with the lives of Peter and Paul in Rome, but it is impossible to vouch for their accuracy.

It is certain that there are no contemporary images of the two Apostles, no more than of Christ or of

His Blessed Mother, but it is beyond doubt that the ancient artists had before them older monuments and followed a traditional type in painting their pictures. Eusebius in the fourth century tells us that they had representations of the two Apostles by Gentile painters, converted by them to the faith. Peter is represented as a middle-sized man with curly hair and a short beard; Paul as short of stature with a bald head and a long beard. The oldest of these medallions in bronze that we know of belongs to the second century. We may suppose that the artist had seen the Apostles, or at least had friends that knew them. Other bronzes of the first half of the third century perpetuated these traditional types. The stained glasses in the cemeteries in the third and fourth century always represent the same types. The figures of the two Apostles may be easily recognized in the frescoes adorning the Roman catacombs. Most of those remaining date from the fourth century.

The above sufficiently shows that the Church of Rome had from the beginning numerous representations of the two apostles. The reason of that cannot be accidental, nor to be found in the fact of a general veneration, but in the common conviction that Rome had been the field of their apostolate; history and archæology confirm it.

The documents and monuments of the Primitive Church in Rome do not only disclose the presence of the two Apostles, but they also furnish clear allusions to Peter's primacy. Christ is often represented in the act of consigning his law, but He invariably hands the sacred volume to Peter; he was looked upon as the custodian of divine revelation by Christ's appointment.

Besides the proofs given above to substantiate a few points of Christian belief, there are many more evidences in the sacred volume to enlighten us on many other practices in the Primitive Church. The following are a few of them:

The necessity of Baptism had been so emphasized by Jesus Christ that we need no tradition to admit that it was from the beginning administered to children. Further, the Church has always held that martyrdom, being the sublime expression of perfect love, was in its efficacy equal to Baptism for the remission of sins, and that when the Baptism of water could not be received, sincere desire took its place.

We have seen the Apostles, Peter and John, administering a sacred rite, by which the Holy Ghost was given to the converts baptized by St. Philip; we call that rite the sacrament of Confirmation.

St. Paul illustrates in his epistles the sacrifice of the New Law and the real presence of Christ under the appearances of bread and wine.

The Apostles had received from Christ the power to bind and to loose, to forgive and to retain sins. They could not use that power, unless the offender submitted the matter, on which they were to pass sentence. It would be absurd and blasphemous to assert that the Apostles did not make use of the sublime power, conferred upon them in favor of sinful humanity. The confession of sins demanded by St.

James (V.16) "one to another" is the confession made to a presbyter, called in to anoint the sick.

Jesus Christ did not remove the penalty of death in the new order of things established by Him, but He has eased the last struggle and sweetened the last agony. He had one of His Apostles to proclaim in writing this great help for both body and soul. We now call that sacred rite Extreme Unction (James V).

As Christ willed that His Church should exist unto the end of time as a visible society, He appointed a ministry, to whom He gave graces commensurate with the obligations, which He placed upon them. By the imposition of hands the Apostles conveyed their powers in whole or in part to their lawful successors.

As Christ had provided special graces to those, whom He sent as the Father had sent Him, so He impressed upon the matrimonial contract the sign of the sacred union between Himself and the Church to perpetuate the human race, all of whom could become His children by adoption. He chose especially the Apostle of the Gentiles to proclaim that sacred institution to the world in writing.

There is not the remotest doubt but that all the above practices were in use in the Primitive Church.

CHAPTER THIRTY-FIRST

THE GREAT GENERAL PERSECUTIONS IN THE DAYS
OF THE APOSTLES

WE do not know the exact number of Christians in the days of St. Peter. We may suppose that there were several thousands. Rome at that time counted about two million inhabitants. The Christian religion in the beginning was not forbidden by law; the profession of it was free. The Roman law recognized the Jewish religion, and it found protectors in Julius Cæsar and Augustus. There was an occasional uprising against them, but always of short duration. In 42 Claudius confirmed all their privileges; he expelled them from Rome in 49, but they soon returned, and in Nero's time there was a great number of them. Their legal freedom extended to the Christians, who, but for a little difference, were looked upon as a Judaic sect. This applied not only to the converts from Judaism, but also to the converts from paganism.

The Jews had in the past often caused an uprising against the Apostles and their converts; they also appealed to the Roman courts to repress them, but their claims, as we have seen, were as a rule disregarded. Claudius expelled from Rome all that were known as Jews, and this included the Christians, but not as such. As the Jews could not move the courts against them, they excited the multitude. The Jewish converts were soon in the minority; the attention of the people was directed to the ever increasing number of pagan converts. The Jews then started a campaign of suspicion, aversion, and hatred against them. In that way the legality of the Christian religion soon disappeared. This led to the dilemma, either recognize it and permit it by law, like the Jewish religion, or proscribe it. Before we explain how some of the emperors solved it, we must briefly review the expansion of the Church at the time Nero came to the throne.

Paul had been the great Apostle in the provinces depending on the empire, but it was Peter's privilege to extend the Church and give the first bishops to the whole of Italy, Gaul, Spain, Africa, Sicily, and the adjacent isles. Local traditions in various parts bear witness to his zeal and to the mission of his disciples. So was Paulinus the first bishop of Lucca, Romulus of Fiesole, Apollinaris of Ravenna, all disciples of St. Peter. Paul on landing at Pozzuoli found Christians there; the first bishop of that place was Patrobas, whom he salutes in his letter to the Romans (XVI.14). In Campania the Christian religion was propagated at an early date. Judging from an inscription found not so long ago we may infer that there were Christians in Pompeii, when that city was buried in 79 beneath the ashes of Vesuvius. Photinus was the first bishop of Benevento,

Priscus of Capua, Aspren of Naples; all disciples of St. Peter. Trophimus was sent by St. Peter as first bishop of Arles in Gaul. There is no doubt but that the chief of the Apostles had propagated the Christian religion in various countries. The greater part of the Roman empire was dotted with Christian communities in the latter part of Nero's reign. He was the first of the ten persecutors of the early days. We will treat of three only; Nero, Domitian, and Trajan; under whose reign the last survivor of the Apostles died.

Nero was the son of Agrippina, the second wife of Claudius. He adopted him and gave him in marriage his own daughter, Octavia. Born in 37 Nero came to the throne in 54. The first years of his reign were auspicious in every way, but then his nobler dispositions were stifled by sensuality and moral perversity. Nero practised his cruelty on his own mother, whom he had his freedmen club to death; he beheaded his wife to whom he owed the throne; he put out of the way in like fashion all that seemed to oppose him. The material welfare of the city declined with the increasing extravagance of Nero; general misery reached its highest, when the terrible conflagration occurred in 64. The best contemporary authorities claim that Nero himself had the city put on fire; thousands perished in it. Bribed informers laid the blame on the Christians. A fierce persecution throughout the empire began. The property of the Christians was confiscated for the building of a new Rome. Tacitus in his Annals gives us the following description of what happened: The disaster happened whether by accident or by fraud on the part of the emperor is uncertain; authors have asserted both. At that time Nero was at Antium, and did not return until the fire threatened his palace and the gardens of Mæcenas. He then extended help to the poor people, but his purpose was fruitless, because the rumor spread that, when the city was on fire, he was singing the destruction of Troja, comparing present ills with past disasters. The fire burnt itself out on the sixth day, but soon broke out again in another part. Nero ambitioned the glory of building a new city under his own name. Tacitus then relates the persecution of the Christians. No human help, no liberality on the part of Nero, no sacrifices offered to the gods, could remove from the emperor the mark of infamy, because it was believed that he had given the order to burn the city. To drown the rumor Nero made semblance of looking for the guilty parties and to torture them in a most atrocious manner. The Christians were pointed out; Christ their founder under the reign of Tiberius was tortured by Pontius Pilate. That dreadful superstition had broken out anew, not only in Judea, the birthplace of that evil, but in Rome itself, where all shame flocks and is held in honor. The first to suffer were those who confessed and then on their betrayal a great multitude were accused of complicity in the fire and condemned by the hatred of mankind. Nero added insult to the dying; he ordered them covered with the skins of wild beasts and to be torn to pieces by wild dogs, or to be nailed to crosses, or to be burnt alive to light up a dark night. Nero offered his gardens for such exhibitions, in which he mingled with the crowd, dressed up as a coachman, or standing on his chariot. A feeling of pity prevailed upon the common people; they felt that those so cruelly treated were not sacrificed for the common good, but to satisfy the vengeance of one.

Writing about the same persecution Suetonius devotes a chapter to the tortures of the Christians, whom he calls a class of people, belonging to a new and wicked superstition.

From Tacitus' account we gather that Nero first proceeded against the Christians for the burning of Rome, and that then the courts outlawed the profession of the Christian religion, and sanctioned the distinction between Christianity and Judaism. Most probably the persecution of Nero did not extend to the Jews, but was restricted to the Christians. The accusations of the Jews had made them odious in the eyes of the masses, and made them an easy target for Nero's flatterers. From that same account we learn that a great multitude of Christians were martyred, but the exact number is unknown. The persecution kept up in all its fury up to Nero's death in 68. The profession of Christianity was looked upon as a crime, and therefore it was persistently persecuted, even when the suspicion about the fire had been removed. It is probable that the persecution extended to the countries close to Rome, but not to the other provinces. We have already explained the martyrdom of

Peter and Paul in the year 67, the year before Nero's **death.** Nero's tyranny approached its overthrow. The Senate declared him an enemy to his country, and sentenced him to the death of a common murderer. He committed suicide in June, 68.

The acts of Nero's reign were rescinded after his death, but the persecution of the Christians remained permissible. The unpopularity of the Jews, and the destruction of the Holy City, deprived the Christians of any protection they might have enjoyed for being mistaken for them.

Between 68 and 81 the Church enjoyed relative peace; then the younger brother of Titus succeeded him on the imperial throne.

Ancient writers tell us that Domitian gave many proofs of cruelty and murdered unjustly many noble and prominent men of the city. He then began to exile a numberless multitude of innocent men of the highest standing for the purpose of confiscating their property. At the end he gave himself out as the heir of Nero's wickedness and of his war and hatred against God. He was the second to start a general persecution against the Christians, although his father, Vespasian, had never attempted anything injurious to them.

Cassius another writer tells us that besides many others, Domitian killed his cousin Flavius Clemens, the consul, with his wife Flavia Domitilla, also a blood relation, for impiety to the gods; many were similarly condemned or had their property confiscated. The causes of this persecution seem to have been the following; Domitian was a cruel tyrant, suspicious and haughty, who claimed for himself the name of lord and god; ostentatiously he promoted the national worship of the Romans. The propagation of Christianity was most displeasing to him, more so as many of his own family adhered to it. Perhaps even the third successor of St. Peter—St. Clement—belonged to it. Many of the noble families had at that time accepted Christianity, as the discovered contemporary tombs in the catacombs prove. Domitian feared the coming of Christ and of His kingdom; he feared that descendants of David and relatives of Christ might endanger his throne. He had them brought from the East to Rome, but when he found out that they were poor and had to support themselves with hard work, as their callous hands showed, he dismissed them. If Domitian was so cruel towards the members of his own family, we may readily imagine how he behaved towards strangers.

It is interesting to see how the primitive Christian nobility of Rome formed a brotherly society with the poor, the slaves of the great metropolis, exemplifying in their lives that true equality, as announced by Christ.

St. John, the last survivor of the twelve Apostles, lived during part of the reign of another famous persecutor of the Church—Trajan.

Trajan succeeded Nerva on January 28, 98. His attitude towards the Christians is best understood through a famous letter of Pliny the younger, prefect of Bithynia, inquiring how to deal with the Christians and from Trajan's answer to it.

The contents of that letter read as follows: It is my duty to refer to you, my Lord, all questions of which I doubt. Who can better dissipate my doubts and instruct my ignorance? I have never assisted at trials of Christians; hence I do not know whether and how to punish them or find them out. I have my serious doubts whether age makes any difference, or whether the weak differ from the strong, and whether they can be forgiven, or cease to be Christians to their advantage, and whether when their name is so far untarnished, misdeeds attributed to them are punishable. Meanwhile I have followed this method in dealing with those that were brought before me: I have asked them whether they were Christians; I have repeated the question three times and always received the same answer; I threatened them, yet they persevered. I had no doubt but that, whatever they said, their stubbornness should be punished. There have been others similarly demented, whom I ordered to be taken to Rome, because they were Roman citizens. There have been various other kinds. I have received an anonymous petition containing the names of those, who denied that they were or had been Christians. At my suggestion they called upon the gods, and they offered wine and incense to thy image, which I had brought together with the statues of the gods; moreover, they cursed Christ. They say that true Christians cannot be induced to do any of these things. I was of the opinion that these should be dismissed. Others have been tried by a judge and confessed that they had been Christians but had ceased to be three or twenty years ago. They affirmed, however, that the sum total of their mistakes was as follows: They were wont to meet on a given day before sunrise; they would sing alternately to Christ as God, and pledge themselves not to commit a crime, not to steal or rob, not to commit adultery, not to deny their faith. After that they could leave, or meet again to take food. They did not assist at the meetings again, after I had forbidden at thy command these superstitions. I thought it necessary to find out the truth from two servant-girls, by submitting them to torture, but all I could discover was a bad and exaggerated superstition. After having explained these facts I take my recourse to thee for advice. Many of all ages, all orders, and of both sexes, are tried or will be. The contagion of this superstition is spread not only in the city, but in the hamlets and in the country; seemingly it can be stayed and corrected. It is apparent that our temples are nearly abandoned, the services seldom repeated, and the victims find no buyers. It is easy to think what a multitude of men could be punished, if need be.

Trajan's answer to the above letter was couched in the following terms: My dear Secundus. Thou hast acted properly in trying those that were brought before thee as Christians. No certain procedure in the matter can be established. There need be no systematic search for them; if they are accused and convicted, they should be punished. If they deny to be Christians and prove their denial by offering to our gods, they can be forgiven after a penance, although the suspicion be that they were formerly Christians. In regard to the anonymous petition, there is no occasion to prosecute; it is a bad example and not limited to our days.

From the two letters we gather that Christianity had very many adherents in Bithynia, in the country as well as in the cities. The emperor restrained the persecution in so far that there was to be no systematic search, and at the same time he officially declared that Christians are outlawed and have no legal existence, and that they may be brought to trial and convicted on the strength of existing laws.

Trajan as a persecutor of the Church had seven successors, the one surpassing the other in cruelty.

We have limited our remarks concerning persecutions to those that were waged against Christianity in the Roman empire. Most of the Apostles were sent to countries independent of the empire; as all of them died martyrs, we may suppose that they and their converts were persecuted.

CHAPTER THIRTY-SECOND

ST. JOHN AND THE END OF THE APOSTOLIC AGE

St. John was called, with Peter and James, a pillar of the Church (Gal. II.9). Among the four Cherubs who in the prophecy of Ezechiel (I.10) represent the four evangelists, St. John has always been likened to the eagle. All the sacred writers have drawn from the source of eternal wisdom; Paul had even been taken up to the third heaven and heard mysterious words; John rose higher and heard in the supreme cause of all the one Word, by whom all has been created. His virginal purity made him an angel in the flesh. He was the patriarch of all the faithful, because he survived all the other Apostles. He was an Apostle, a bishop, a doctor, an evangelist, and a prophet. He was a martyr, because he endured with Christ all the horrors of the crucifixion, so far as he was able, and because he suffered the tortures of death, from which he was saved by miracle. He was not beheaded like Paul, nor crucified like Peter, but he was cast into a cauldron of boiling oil. Like the three children in the Babylonian furnace, he escaped unhurt with renewed vigor and beauty. This happened in Rome at the Latin gate under the reign of Domitian. At the same time John was scourged and had his head shaved as a mark of infamy, before he was sent into exile to the island of Patmos, whose inhabitants he converted. The martyr's death was the chalice which Christ promised to all His Apostles. John alludes to it in his Apocalypse (I.9). John was the Apostle of love all through his life. He gave proofs of it not only by founding churches everywhere, but also by taking an individual interest in the most degraded of sinners. Eusebius has left us an illustration of it in the case of a young man, whom John had recommended to the special care of a bishop, and who through bad company had become the chief of a band of robbers. On a visit to the bishop, John demanded the young man, the soul of a brother. The bishop regretfully had to confess that he was dead to God and had become a robber chief. John on hearing this, tore his garments, burst out in sighs and ironically remarked to the bishop that he was a fine guardian of his brother. He ordered that he procure a horse and a guide. John mounted the horse and left the city in haste. The guards of the robbers' camp saw him coming. John demanded to see their chief. He came fully armed, but on noticing his spiritual father, and ashamed of himself he took to flight. John forgetting his age (he was over ninety) spurred his horse and went after him and cried out: My son, why avoid your father? why be afraid of an unarmed old man? Fear not, you have still the hope of life; as Christ died for us, I am willing to die for you. Halt! Have confidence in me, because Christ sent me. The wretch heard him, halted, with downcast eyes threw away his arms, and fell at the knees of the old man, who came to him. His sighs and his tears betokened sorrow and enabled St. John to restore him to the communion of the Church.

After Christ had foretold to Peter by what manner of death he would glorify God, Peter noticed John and he asked Christ what would become of him. Christ answered: "So I will have him to remain till I come" (Jo. XXI.23). Some writers in the remote past have drawn from these words of Christ the conclusion that St. John, like Henoch and Elias, is not dead, but has like them his mortal body somewhere in earthly paradise, and will return with them at the end of the world to preach against the Antichrist, who will put him to death. They add that by a special privilege he sees and enjoys God. Most of the ancient writers, however, assert and the whole Church admits that St. John is dead and reigns with Christ and the other Blessed in heaven.

We know that the Church, like the twilight and the sun, gradually grows to the perfect knowledge of the mysteries of faith. Hence the sacred writers of the New Testament have written more clearly, more distinctly and sublimely than Moses and the Prophets of the Old Testament. St. John was the author of the last inspired book and added the crown to the work.

The love of God and of the neighbor was the inspiration of his whole life. In extreme old age, when unable to make long speeches he would repeat at all the meetings of the faithful: "My little children, love one another." When asked by his disciples why he always repeated the same, he gave the following answer worthy of the Apostle of love: Because it is the commandment of Christ, and if it be kept, it is sufficient.

After removing Domitian from the throne, the Senate selected Nerva as emperor, with the consent of the army; he reigned from 96 to 98. On the advice of the Senate the new emperor rescinded the acts of Domitian and recalled those who had been sent in exile. In consequence of this general amnesty St. John was released from the island of Patmos, and he returned to Ephesus. He brought order out of the chaos created by the persecution of Domitian, and by the heresies, chiefly of the Cerinthians and the Ebionites, appointed proper ministers for the various churches of Asia. He lived in Ephesus up to the end of his life between 101 and 104, and was buried near that city.

St. John, being the last of the inspired writers, could have left us a catalogue of all the inspired writers of the Old and the New Testament, but he did not. He knew that it was safe to leave that to the teaching Church under the guidance of the Holy Spirit, and that those appointed to rule the church of God would be able at all times to separate the cockle from the wheat.

From the remotest days of the Christian era other writings than those in the Canon of Holy Scriptures have been circulated and attributed to the Apostles. This was partly due to local traditions, partly to a pious fraud used for the purpose of adding authority and influence.

With the last Apostle, disappearing from the scene of this world, the apostolic age closed.

The Lord is ever merciful; His grace and His power will be for ever manifested in His elect, but in the future His grace will not be poured out through the fulness of miracles, as in the days of the Apostles. Human prudence will fail in all its calculations; the wisdom of the world will appear foolishness. A religion humbling pride by its mysteries, mortifying the senses, imposing self-abnegation, predicting persecution, and promising great indeed but invisible joys; a religion preached by poor and ignorant Galileans will be embraced by Jew and Gentile. The Jew will give up his belief in the earthly kingdom of the Messiah, the Greek the shadow of pagan philosophy, Rome will destroy its gods and bend the knee to the Nazarene.

Who can deny the visible intervention of Christ in the institution, of which He is the invisible Head?

THE END

INDEX

A

Apostles scourged, 54; dispersion of, 110; little known, 71; work and death, 71; writings, 72

Ananias, 79

Agabus the Prophet, 119

Annas, 50

Ananias and Saphira, 40

Apostolic age close of, 291

B

Barnabas, 82, 114, 39

Bible or written word—New Testament did not exist first years, 103; not necessary, 103; why New Testament was written, 103; Inspired writers, 103; first Christians had none, 105; difficulties in interpreting, 107; Bible and oral Tradition, 108

Baptism, 34

C

Church Perfect society, 1; independent, 3; visible head after Christ, 8; one, 30; differs from Synagogue, 35; economic organization, 39; Persecutions of, 46; hierarchy, 94; Bishops, Priests and Deacons, 94; at Ephesus, 178; Primitive churches, 269

Cemeteries, 270

Christians dispersed, 57; name, 113; religious life of first, 31

Confirmation, 68

Chronology, 70

Christianity its demands, 29; challenge from Judaism, 51

Caiphas, 50

Communion frequent, 37

Ceremonies, 265

Collections, 45

D

Damascus, 76

Dates of important events, 91

Deacons ordination, 43, 99

Deaconesses, 100

Denis St., 171

E

Eunuch of Ethiopia, 69

Eucharist, 36, 265; Sacrifice, 266

Epicureans, 167

G

Gamaliel, 53

Gentiles first efforts among them, 85

H

Herods, 121

Heresies Simon the Magician, 257; Gnostics, 259; Judaizers,

293

languages, 26; repeated, 28
Philip, the deacon, 64
Pharisees, 47
Popes of first century, St. Peter, 247; St. Limus, 248; St. Cletus, 249; St. Clement, 249; recognised during lifetime of St. John, 250

R

Revelation Freedom of accepting, 29
Rome burning of, 224

S

Sacraments, 275
Sadducees, 47
Samaritans schismatics, 64; converts, 66
Sanhedrim, 49

Sergius Paul, 131
Simon the Magician, 66
Soothsayers and Spiritists, 161
Stephen first martyr, 55
Stoics, 167
Sunday celebration of, 187

T

Thomas St., 60
Temple one, 33
Thecla, 136

W

Women abettors of heresy, 135
Worship public, 264
Writers of New Testament, St. Matthew, 231; St. Mark, 233; St. Luke, 234; St. John, 235; St. Paul, 238; St. James, 240; St. Peter, 242; St. Jude, 244

If you have enjoyed this book, consider making your next selection from among the following . . .

Prices guaranteed through December 31, 1989.

The Two Divine Promises. Fr. Hoppe................ 1.00
St. Teresa of Ávila. William Thomas Walsh...........16.50
Isabella of Spain—The Last Crusader. Wm. T. Walsh....16.50
Characters of the Inquisition. Wm. T. Walsh...........10.00
Philip II. William Thomas Walsh. H.B...............30.00
Blood-Drenched Altars—Cath. Comment. Hist. Mexico..16.50
Self-Abandonment to Divine Providence. de Caussade...15.00
Way of the Cross. Liguorian....................... .60
Way of the Cross. Franciscan...................... .60
Modern Saints—Their Lives & Faces. Ann Ball........15.00
Saint Michael and the Angels. Approved Sources....... 4.50
Dolorous Passion of Our Lord. Anne C. Emmerich.....12.50
Our Lady of Fatima's Peace Plan from Heaven. Booklet. .40
Divine Favors Granted to St. Joseph. Pere Binet........ 3.50
St. Joseph Cafasso—Priest of the Gallows. St. J. Bosco.. 2.00
Catechism of the Council of Trent. McHugh/Callan.....20.00
Padre Pio—The Stigmatist. Fr. Charles Carty..........11.00
Why Squander Illness? Frs. Rumble & Carty.......... 1.50
Fatima—The Great Sign. Francis Johnston............. 6.00
Heliotropium—Conformity of Human Will to Divine.... 9.00
Charity for the Suffering Souls. Fr. John Nageleisen....12.50
Devotion to the Sacred Heart of Jesus. Verheylezoon....10.50
Religious Liberty. Michael Davies................... 1.00
Sermons on Prayer. St. Francis de Sales.............. 3.00
Sermons on Our Lady. St. Francis de Sales........... 8.00
Sermons for Lent. St. Francis de Sales............... 8.00
Fundamentals of Catholic Dogma. Ott................16.50
Litany of the Blessed Virgin Mary. (100 cards)........ 4.00
Who Is Padre Pio? Radio Replies Press............... 1.00
Child's Bible History. Knecht...................... 2.50
The Life of Christ. 4 Vols. H.B. Anne C. Emmerich....50.00
St. Anthony—The Wonder Worker of Padua. Stoddard... 2.50
The Precious Blood. Fr. Faber..................... 9.00
The Holy Shroud & Four Visions. Fr. O'Connell....... 1.50
Clean Love in Courtship. Fr. Lawrence Lovasik........ 2.00
The Prophecies of St. Malachy. Peter Bander.......... 3.50
The Secret of the Rosary. St. Louis De Montfort....... 1.00
The History of Antichrist. Rev. P. Huchede........... 2.00
Where We Got the Bible. Fr. Henry Graham.......... 4.00
Hidden Treasure—Holy Mass. St. Leonard........... 3.00
Imitation of the Sacred Heart of Jesus. Fr. Arnoudt.....12.00
The Life & Glories of St. Joseph. Edward Thompson...11.00

At your bookdealer or direct from the publisher.

Prices guaranteed through December 31, 1989.

NOTES

NOTES